CONTENTS

About
Dr. David Jeremiah
and Turning Point

D r. David Jeremiah is the founder of Turning Point, a ministry committed to providing Christians with sound Bible teaching relevant to today's changing times through radio and television broadcasts, audio series, books, and live events. Dr. Jeremiah's common-sense teaching on topics such as family, prayer, worship, angels, and biblical prophecy forms the foundation of Turning Point.

David and his wife, Donna, reside in El Cajon, California, where he serves as the senior pastor of Shadow Mountain Community Church. David and Donna have four children and twelve grandchildren.

In 1982, Dr. Jeremiah brought the same solid teaching to San Diego television that he shares weekly with his congregation. Shortly thereafter, Turning Point expanded its ministry to radio. Dr. Jeremiah's inspiring messages can now be heard worldwide on radio, television, and the Internet.

Because Dr. Jeremiah desires to know his listening audience, he travels nationwide holding ministry rallies and spiritual enrichment conferences that touch the hearts and lives of many people. According to Dr. Jeremiah, "At some point in time, everyone reaches a turning point; and for every person, that moment is unique, an experience to hold onto forever. There's so much changing in today's world that sometimes it's difficult to choose the right path. Turning Point offers people an understanding of God's Word as well as the opportunity to make a difference in their lives."

Dr. Jeremiah has authored numerous books, including *Escape the Coming Night* (Revelation), *The Handwriting on the Wall* (Daniel), *Overcoming Loneliness, Prayer—The Great Adventure, God in You* (Holy Spirit), *When Your World Falls Apart, My Heart's Desire, 31 Days to Happiness—Searching for Heaven on Earth, Captured by Grace, Grace Givers, Signs of Life, What in the World Is Going On?, The Coming Economic Armageddon, I Never Thought I'd See the Day!, God Loves You: He Always Has—He Always Will, What Are You Afraid Of?, Agents of the Apocalypse,* and *RESET—Ten Steps to Spiritual Renewal.*

HOW TO USE THIS STUDY GUIDE

The purpose of this Turning Point study guide is to reinforce Dr. David Jeremiah's dynamic, in-depth teaching and to aid the reader in applying biblical truth to his or her daily life. This study guide is designed to be used in conjunction with Dr. Jeremiah's *Overcoming Loneliness* audio series, but it may also be used by itself for personal or group study.

STRUCTURE OF THE LESSONS

Each lesson is based on one of the messages in the *Overcoming Loneliness* compact disc series and focuses on specific passages in the Bible. Each lesson is composed of the following elements:

- *Outline*

The outline at the beginning of the lesson gives a clear, concise picture of the topic being studied and provides a helpful framework for readers as they listen to Dr. Jeremiah's teaching.

- *Overview*

The overview summarizes Dr. Jeremiah's teaching on the passage being studied in the lesson. Readers should refer to the Scripture passages in their own Bibles as they study the overview. Unless otherwise indicated, Scripture verses quoted are taken from the New King James Version.

- *Personal and Group Application Questions*

This section contains a variety of questions designed to help readers dig deeper into the lesson and the Scriptures, and to apply the lesson to their daily lives. For Bible study groups or Sunday school classes, these questions will provide a springboard for group discussion and interaction.

- *Did You Know?*

This section presents a fascinating fact, historical note, or insight that adds a point of interest to the preceding lesson.

PERSONAL STUDY

Thank you for selecting *Overcoming Loneliness* for your current study. The lessons in this study guide were created to help you gain fresh insights into God's Word and develop new perspectives on topics you may have previously studied. Each lesson is designed to challenge your thinking, and help you grow in your knowledge of Christ. During your study, it is our prayer that you will discover how biblical truth affects every aspect of your life and your relationship with Christ will be strengthened.

When you commit to completing this study guide, try to set apart a time, daily or weekly, to read through the lessons without distraction. Have your Bible nearby when you read the study guide, so you're ready to look up verses if you need to. If you want to use a notebook to write down your thoughts, be sure to have that handy as well. Take your time to think through and answer the questions. If you plan on reading the study guide with a small group, be sure to read ahead and be prepared to take part in the weekly discussions.

LEADER'S GUIDE

Thank you for your commitment to lead a group through *Overcoming Loneliness*. Being a leader has its own rewards. You may discover that your walk with the Lord deepens through this experience. Throughout the study guide, your group will explore new topics and review study questions that encourage thought-provoking group discussion.

The lessons in this study guide are suitable for Sunday school classes, small-group studies, elective Bible studies, or home Bible study groups. Each lesson is structured to provoke thought and help you grow in your knowledge and understanding of God. There are multiple components in this section that can help you structure your lessons and discussion time, so make sure you read and consider each one.

Before You Begin

Before you begin each meeting, make sure you and your group are well-versed with the content of the chapter. Every person should have his or her own study guide so they can follow along and write in the study guide if need be. When possible, the study guide should be used with the corresponding compact disc series. You may wish to assign the study guide lesson as homework prior to the meeting of the group and then use the meeting time to listen to the CD and discuss the lesson.

To ensure that everyone has a chance to participate in the discussion, the ideal size for a group is around eight to ten people. If there are more than ten people, try to break up the bigger group into smaller subgroups. Make sure the members are committed to participating each week, as this will help create stability and help you better prepare the structure of the meeting.

At the beginning of the study each week, start the session with a question to challenge group members to think about the issues you will be discussing. The members can answer briefly, but the goal is to have an idea in their mind as you go over the lesson. This allows the group members to become engaged and ready to interact with the group.

After reviewing the lesson, try to initiate a free-flowing discussion. Invite group members to bring questions and insights they may have discovered to the next meeting, especially if they were unsure of the meaning of some parts of the lesson. Be prepared to discuss how biblical truth applies to the world we live in today.

Weekly Preparation

As the group leader, here are a few things you can do to prepare for each meeting:

- Choose whether or not you will play the CD message during your small group session.

  If you decide to play the CD message from Dr. Jeremiah as part of the meeting, you will need to adjust the group time accordingly.

- Make sure you are thoroughly familiar with the material in the lesson.

  Make sure you understand the content of the lesson so you know how to structure group time and you are prepared to lead group discussion.

- Decide, ahead of time, which questions you plan to discuss.

  Depending on how much time you have each week, you may not be able to reflect on every question. Select specific questions which you feel will evoke the best discussion.

- Take prayer requests.

  At the end of your discussion, take prayer requests from your group members and pray for each other.

Structuring the Discussion Time

If you need help in organizing your time when planning your group Bible study, here are two schedules, for sixty minutes and ninety minutes, which can give you a structure for the lesson:

Option 1 (Listen to Audio CD)	60 Minutes	90 Minutes
Welcome: Members arrive and get settled.	N/A	5 minutes
Getting Started Question: Prepares the group for interacting with one another.	Welcome and Getting Started 5 minutes	15 minutes
Message: Listen to the audio CD.	40 minutes	40 minutes
Discussion: Discuss group study questions.	10 minutes	25 minutes
Prayer and Application: Final application for the week and prayer before dismissal.	5 minutes	5 minutes

Option 2 (No Audio CD)	60 Minutes	90 Minutes
Welcome: Members arrive and get settled.	5 minutes	10 minutes
Getting Started Question: Prepares the group for interacting with one another.	10 minutes	10 minutes
Message: Review the lesson.	15 minutes	25 minutes
Discussion: Discuss group study questions.	25 minutes	35 minutes
Prayer and Application: Final application for the week and prayer before dismissal.	5 minutes	10 minutes

As the group leader, it is up to you to keep track of the time and keep things moving along according to your schedule. If your group is having a good discussion, don't feel the need to stop and move on to the next question. Remember, the purpose is to pull together ideas, and share unique insights on the lesson. Make time each week to discuss how to apply these truths to living for Christ today.

The purpose of discussion is for everyone to participate, but don't be concerned if certain group members are more quiet—they may be internally reflecting on the questions and need time to process their ideas before they can share them.

Group Dynamics

Leading a group study can be a rewarding experience for you and your group members—but that doesn't mean there won't be challenges. Certain members may feel uncomfortable discussing topics that they consider very personal, and might be afraid of being called on. Some members might have disagreements on specific issues. To help prevent these scenarios, consider the following ground rules:

- If someone has a question that may seem off topic, suggest that it is discussed at another time, or ask the group if they are okay with addressing that topic.

- If someone asks a question you don't know the answer to, confess that you don't know and move on. If you feel comfortable, invite other group members to give their opinions, or share their comments based on personal experience.

- If you feel like a couple of people are talking much more than others, direct questions to people who may not have shared yet. You could even ask the more dominating members to help draw out the quiet ones.

- When there is a disagreement, encourage the group members to process the matter in love. Invite members from opposing sides to evaluate their opinions and consider the ideas of the other members. Lead the group through Scripture that addresses the topic, and look for common ground.

When issues arise, remind your group to think of Scripture: "Love one another" (John 13:34), "If it is possible, as much as depends on you, live peaceably with all men" (Romans 12:18), and "Be quick to listen, slow to speak and slow to become angry" (James 1:19, NIV).

For Continuing Study

For a complete listing of Dr. Jeremiah's materials for personal and group study call 1-800-947-1993, go online to www.DavidJeremiah.org, or write to Turning Point, P.O. Box 3838, San Diego, CA 92163.

Dr. Jeremiah's *Turning Point* program is currently heard or viewed around the world on radio, television, and the Internet in English. *Momento Decisivo*, the Spanish translation of Dr. Jeremiah's messages, can be heard on radio in every Spanish speaking country in the world. The television broadcast is also broadcast by satellite throughout the Middle East with Arabic subtitles.

Contact Turning Point for radio and television program times and stations in your area, or visit our website at www.DavidJeremiah.org/stationlocator.

OVERCOMING LONELINESS

INTRODUCTION

An August 6, 2006, Associated Press wire story took a fresh look at a disturbing trend in America's social fabric: loneliness. We have never been more populous (around the 320 million mark) and never more connected (email, cell phones, instant messaging, social media, text messaging, overnight deliveries). But ironically, we have never been lonelier. The article cited John Powell, a psychologist at a University of Illinois counseling center who noted that it is increasingly common for incoming freshmen to use electronic means to communicate with others rather than engaging in face-to-face exchanges. Dorm rooms become electronic communication bunkers that students don't need to leave in order to feel connected. But the human element is missing.

Here's another disturbing trend: The latest U.S. census figures show that more than one-fourth of the nation's households (34.75 million) are occupied by only one person. This is an increase from only ten percent in 1950. But this may be the most disturbing trend: A June 2006 study by the American Sociological Review reported that the average American had only two close friends with whom they could discuss an important matter. In 1985, ten percent of the U.S. population said they didn't have a single close friend in whom they could confide. In 2004, that number more than doubled to 25 percent of the population. Another nineteen percent of the population said (in 2004) they had only one close friend, often reported to be a spouse. If that spouse dies, the person is left isolated and alone without a social support network.

The changing social structures of our modern society have caused us to be less dependent on one another. There was a time when people didn't own, or couldn't afford to provide for themselves, all the goods and services they needed in life. They were much more dependent on extended family, friends, and neighbors which resulted in social networks being formed and loneliness being a rarity rather than a common occurrence. But today, affluence allows most Americans to own most of what they need. We are less dependent on others for life's necessities, so we stay sealed in our climate-controlled homes, trying to recoup from the stress of our busy lifestyles. And loneliness is the result.

Sadly, we don't recognize loneliness until it's too late. It is a creeping condition that slowly becomes part of our life. Our busyness keeps us distracted—and when we do feel lonely, the television and Internet are always on and able to fill the void.

But there isn't supposed to be a void! "Lonely" is not the way God created man to live. He has provided companionship on two levels for every human being: human and divine. First, God established social networks as part of His created design: marriage, family, extended family, church, community, and para-church and para-community groups that organize around tasks and missions. Every human being who wants to live a healthy life can be plugged in to these horizontal networks.

But there is another kind of relationship for which humans were created: a vertical relationship with the God who says, "I created you for myself; I love you; I want you to know Me; I want to walk with you daily; I will never leave you nor forsake you." Even if our horizontal, human networks are lacking, God has provided a preventive shield against the debilitating effects of loneliness: a relationship with Himself.

In this study guide you will learn how to defeat the enemy called isolation and overcome loneliness at the many horizontal levels of life. But you will also be reminded of God's heavenly cure for loneliness—a relationship with Him through Jesus Christ. There may be times when we are alone in terms of personal contacts and relationships, but we need never be lonely again.

THE LONELY SERVANT

The Book of Jeremiah

*In this lesson we're introduced to the prophet Jeremiah,
a leader who struggled with loneliness.*

OUTLINE

No one is exempt from circumstances leading to discouragement.
The challenge is not to live an insulated or isolated life, but to be
prepared to keep discouragement from turning to despair. Conviction,
confidence, and commitment can lead to steadfastness in life.

I. **The Reasons for Jeremiah's Loneliness**
   A. He Was Depressed by the Decline of the Nation
   B. He Was Disheartened by the Disinterest of the People
   C. He Was Distressed by the Desertion of His Friends

II. **The Reasons for Jeremiah's Steadfastness**
   A. He Had a Conviction of His Calling
   B. He Had a Confidence in His Companion
   C. He Had a Commitment Beyond His Circumstances
   D. He Had a Cause of Celebration in the Midst of Difficulty

T here are many different kinds of loneliness that people face. There is the kind that comes when we lose a loved one—an aching loneliness in the heart. There is the kind of loneliness that comes from being separated from friends. I've often heard missionaries speak of facing a crisis while living on the opposite side of the world, apart from all friends and family. But there is also a kind of loneliness that we can experience in the midst of a crowd. It is the loneliness that comes to those who have been called to stand alone. This sort of loneliness occurs most often with leaders, but it can take place in the life of any Christian who feels called to take a position that does not meet the approval of the majority.

One follower of God carried on a public ministry for fifty years; the entire time, he felt alone and unappreciated. He watched terrible things happen to God's people through the reign of five different kings, and saw disorder and dissension tear his nation apart. This prophet of God observed the nation of Israel as it turned its back on God, and he was able to see firsthand the discontent and despair that came over his generation as a result. He ministered in the land of Judah as an unpopular, opposed, condemned, ridiculed, and scorned man. On one occasion, he was stoned and thrown out of his hometown. Another time he was beaten as a public disgrace. One time he was imprisoned, thrown into a pit, and left for dead by those in charge. This man was so lonely that he wrote a whole book of funeral poems to describe his lamentations at the destruction of the Holy City. This is the lonely, hurting man we know as Jeremiah.

THE REASONS FOR JEREMIAH'S LONELINESS

The prophet Jeremiah ministered during the last forty years of Judah's history, from the thirteenth year of King Josiah to the destruction of the nation. In my estimation, he is the loneliest man to walk through the pages of the Old Testament. What caused him such loneliness was his depression over the decline of his country. He described it this way: "An astonishing and horrible thing has been committed in the land: the prophets prophesy falsely, and the priests rule by their *own* power; and My people love *to have it* so. But what will you do in the end?" (Jeremiah 5:30–31). There was corruption and decline in Israel, and the people took a fancy to it.

He Was Depressed by the Decline of the Nation

In Jeremiah 8:20 we read, "The harvest is past, the summer is ended, and we are not saved!" You usually see this used as a missionary verse, but it is the heart cry of a prophet who has looked upon a once great nation and seen its destruction looming. A whole generation of people had fallen away from their godly moorings, and the nation was in decline. In fact, one of the preeminent words in the book of Jeremiah is the word "backslide":

- "Your own wickedness will correct you, and your *backslidings* will rebuke you" (2:19).
- "The LORD said also to me in the days of Josiah the king: 'Have you seen what *backsliding* Israel has done?'" (3:6)
- "Then I saw that for all the causes for which *backsliding* Israel had committed adultery, I had put her away and given her a certificate of divorce; yet her treacherous sister Judah did not fear, but went and played the harlot also" (3:8).
- "Return, you *backsliding* children, *and* I will heal your backslidings" (3:22).
- "Therefore a lion from the forest shall slay them, a wolf of the deserts shall destroy them; a leopard will watch over their cities. Everyone who goes out from there shall be torn in pieces, because their transgressions are many; their *backslidings* have increased" (5:6).
- "O LORD, though our iniquities testify against us, do it for Your name's sake; for our *backslidings* are many, we have sinned against You" (14:7).

Jeremiah, the righteous prophet of God, watched as his nation slid into decline. He continued to preach judgment unto the people, but he knew when he began his ministry that no one would listen. They ignored his words. Imagine the heart of a man of God who cries out against unrighteousness and the people refuse to heed his message. Jeremiah was awfully lonely as he watched his nation slide toward the abyss.

He Was Disheartened by the Disinterest of the People

Jeremiah is sometimes called the "weeping prophet," for he spent much time in tears. "Oh, that my head were waters, and my eyes a fountain of tears, that I might weep day and night for the slain of the daughter of my people," he cried in chapter 9, verse 1. "But if you will not hear it, my soul will weep in secret for *your* pride; my eyes will weep bitterly and run down with tears, because the LORD'S flock has been taken captive" (13:17).

The prophet was crying because the people would not listen to his message. They were not interested in the truth of God, and the prophet's only response was to weep at their disinterest. "Let my eyes flow with tears night and day, and let them not cease; for the virgin daughter of my people has been broken with a mighty stroke, with a very severe blow" (14:17).

In the book of Lamentations, Jeremiah repeated those same feelings, noting at the very start of the book,

The princess among the provinces has become a slave! She weeps bitterly in the night, her tears *are* on her cheeks; among all her lovers she has none to comfort *her*. All her friends have dealt treacherously with her; they have become her enemies (1:1–2).

The prophet would then say of himself, "My eyes fail with tears, my heart is troubled; my bile is poured on the ground because of the destruction of the daughter of my people" (2:11). Their rejection of the Lord had broken his heart. As Jeremiah concerned himself with the judgment and destruction of Israel, all he could do was cry. The tears poured from his eyes because no one would listen to his message.

He Was Distressed by the Desertion of His Friends

Jeremiah stood alone in calling the nation to repentance. Lamentations 1:20–21 records that he was deserted by everyone, and some even prayed for his defeat:

See, O LORD, that I *am* in distress; my soul is troubled; my heart is overturned within me, for I have been very rebellious. Outside the sword bereaves, at home *it is* like death. They have heard that I sigh, *but* no one comforts me. All my enemies have heard of my trouble; they are glad that You have done *it*.

This man was deserted for proclaiming the truth. Back in Jeremiah 15:17–18 are some sad and lonely words:

I did not sit in the assembly of the mockers, nor did I rejoice; I sat alone because of Your hand, for You have filled me with indignation. Why is my pain perpetual and my wound incurable, *which* refuses to be healed? Will you surely be to me like an unreliable stream, *as* waters *that* fail?

He was deserted and alone, standing in the breach of a nation deteriorating, crying out the words God had called him to preach, but no one heard him. The friends who should have stood by his side deserted him, and you can feel the ache in his heart as he writes these words:

> Cursed *be* the day in which I was born! Let the day not be blessed in which my mother bore me! Let the man *be* cursed who brought news to my father, saying, "A male child has been born to you!" making him very glad. And let that man be like the cities which the LORD overthrew, and did not relent; let him hear the cry in the morning and the shouting at noon, because he did not kill me from the womb, that my mother might have been my grave, and her womb always enlarged *with me*. Why did I come forth from the womb to see labor and sorrow, that my days should be consumed with shame? (20:14–18)

This is a man who has hit bottom. He was so discouraged that he wished he'd never been born. It was as though one day it was too much for him. He felt sorry for himself and cried out in despair. Most of us have experienced days like that. There isn't a mature person alive who hasn't felt that sort of agony at times. It got so bad that Jeremiah wanted to run away: "Oh, that I had in the wilderness a lodging place for travelers; that I might leave my people, and go from them! For they *are* all adulterers, an assembly of treacherous men" (9:2). If you have ever been in leadership, you can probably relate to Jeremiah's feelings. He just wants to find a motel out in the desert so that he can run away and hide. Several years ago, someone wrote a book that described why leaders get to the point of quitting. The author described his life like a computer: You push one button and a sermon comes out; you push another and counseling comes out; you push another and a night with the family comes out. It was as though his life were programmed, and he had lost all control. With that feeling came a desire to quit. But Jeremiah never quit. Though he was depressed and in a desperate situation, he stayed true to his task.

THE REASONS FOR JEREMIAH'S STEADFASTNESS

It would have been easy for Jeremiah to throw in the towel, but he didn't. You see, despair wasn't his only emotion. In Jeremiah 20:7–9 we read,

O LORD, You induced me, and I was persuaded; You are stronger than I, and have prevailed. I am in derision daily; everyone mocks me. For when I spoke, I cried out; I shouted, "Violence and plunder!" Because the word of the LORD was made to me a reproach and a derision daily. Then I said, "I will not make mention of Him, nor speak anymore in His name." But *His word* was in my heart like a burning fire shut up in my bones; I was weary of holding *it* back, and I could not.

In other words, Jeremiah got to the point where he felt like keeping his mouth shut and not saying anything else, so distressed was he with the fact that his preaching didn't seem to be accomplishing anything. But he couldn't do it, for the Word of God was "in his bones." He just had to let it out. God's message demanded to be heard. As Paul put it in the New Testament, "Woe is me if I do not preach the gospel!" (1 Corinthians 9:16)

He Had a Conviction of His Calling

Jeremiah wanted out of his job, but he couldn't leave it. He knew he was called to preach repentance to Israel. He wanted to quit, but there was something greater than himself driving him forward. God had called him to the job of preaching, put him in place, and implanted His Word within Jeremiah. No matter how much he wanted to get away from it, he had to continue because it was God who had given him the task.

Have you ever read about Jeremiah's call? God told him, "Before I formed you in the womb I knew you; before you were born I sanctified you; I ordained you a prophet to the nations.... For you shall go to all to whom I send you, and whatever I command you, you shall speak" (1:5, 7). Notice the prominence of the perpendicular pronoun "I": "I formed you . . . I knew you . . . I sanctified you . . . I ordained you. . . . I command you." Jeremiah knew he wasn't in Israel by his own design; he was there because God had placed him there.

My father was a preacher, and he once told me, "David, if you can do anything else besides preach, do it." I thought that was a strange piece of advice coming from a man who had prayed for years that I'd feel called to the ministry, but I understand what he meant. Don't go into the ministry unless you are absolutely certain God has called you to it. Because if you are called by God, you can't really do anything else. I think one of the reasons we have seen so many ministry dropouts in recent years is because a lot of people don't know if they are called. The first test is always to question the call. The problems are great, and the pressure is on, and people think, "Maybe God hasn't called me." But Jeremiah stayed true through his years of ministry because he had the conviction of his calling.

He Had a Confidence in His Companion

Right after Jeremiah talked about the fact that he couldn't refrain from preaching, he went on to talk about his faith in God. "But the LORD *is* with me as a mighty, awesome One. Therefore my persecutors will stumble, and will not prevail" (20:11). You want to have the Lord with you when you face tough times and tough people. He is your comforter and encourager; if your enemies are against God's righteousness, you've got a mighty and awesome God on your side. Jeremiah knew he didn't face his problems alone. He certainly had his moments of weakness, and maybe felt sorry for himself at times. But he didn't give in to those feelings because in the midst of the battle, he knew the mighty Lord was standing next to him. He was confident of His companionship.

This was the same Lord who had said to him, "Do not be afraid of their faces, for I *am* with you to deliver you" (1:8). God also had revealed to Jeremiah, "'For I know the thoughts that I think toward you,' says the LORD, 'thoughts of peace and not of evil, to give you a future and a hope'" (29:11).

The great New England preacher, Jonathan Edwards, in his final hour on this earth, said goodbye to his family, then turned his head to his pillow and declared, "Now where is Jesus of Nazareth, my true and never failing friend?" He said it as though he expected the Lord to walk bodily through the door; within moments, Edwards was ushered into the eternal presence of the Lord. When we feel discouraged and under the pile, we need to look around and see Who is with us—the Almighty God of heaven—and be encouraged.

He Had a Commitment Beyond His Circumstances

Blessed *is* the man who trusts in the LORD, and whose hope is the LORD. For he shall be like a tree planted by the waters, which spreads out its roots by the river, and will not fear when heat comes; but its leaf will be green, and will not be anxious in the year of drought, nor will cease from yielding fruit (17:7–8).

The person who loves God is like a tree with deep roots. During a drought, when all the other trees are perishing, that tree will remain healthy and strong. There is no anxiety, for the commitment of that tree reaches beyond the circumstances of the storm. If we are to succeed in the midst of trouble, and if we are not to quit when the going gets tough, we need to get our roots down deep into the Lord, establishing a commitment in Christ that goes beyond our circumstances. As the apostle Paul put it, "And let us not grow weary while doing good, for in due season we shall reap if we do not lose heart" (Galatians 6:9).

He Had a Cause of Celebration in the Midst of Difficulty

The last thing that wouldn't let Jeremiah quit is a verse that seems almost out of context in this very sad and doleful book. It's chapter 20, verse 13, right after that verse about the Lord being a terribly mighty one. "Sing to the LORD! Praise the LORD! For He has delivered the life of the poor from the hand of evildoers."

In the midst of all of these troubles and difficulties, Jeremiah could still find something to sing about and some encouragement to praise the Lord. Most of the book is filled with difficulty and sorrow, crying out to God, but here in the midst of all of that is a verse that pops out of the text about having a cause of celebration even in the midst of difficulty.

Happiness and joy will raise the threshold of pain. When you are filled with the joy of the Lord, the hurts around you don't touch you quite so quickly. That's one reason I am so deeply committed to music. Music literally raises the threshold of pain in my life and in yours. God uses music to assuage my soul, bring me up out of the dumps. Saul required David to play on his harp to raise the threshold of his pain and depression, and bring him up out of it. That's what music does in all of our hearts. Nehemiah 8:10 says, "The joy of the LORD is your strength."

Most of Jeremiah's book is filled with difficulty and sorrow; in the midst of it all, the prophet could still trust in the Almighty God. When we encounter difficulty, we can look at our circumstances and be discouraged, or we can turn and look at God. He loves us more than we can know and will never allow us to go through anything that is not for our own good. He is over and above our circumstances. Don't quit!

1. Jeremiah is a biblical example of suffering through loneliness. Where does your own loneliness come from?

   a. What causes your loneliness to be strong on some days, and bearable, even weak, on other days?

   b. How do you endure the roller coaster of emotions?

   c. What seemed to cause Jeremiah's loneliness and resultant agony?

   d. What examples of endurance can you take from Jeremiah's life?

2. As you learned from Jeremiah, loneliness can be caused by following God's calling on your life. Jeremiah was instructed to preach repentance to a rebellious nation. Even though his heart broke for the nation of Israel, what kept him going? (Jeremiah 20:9)

3. Loneliness can be prevalent in leadership. Do you know any leaders who have chosen to stand alone in order to follow where God was leading them?

   a. Have you had to endure standing alone after choosing to follow God? What were the circumstances?

   b. Were there lessons from your past that prepared you to stand alone and endure the heartache that would come?

   c. Have you been a lonely leader? What have you needed to walk away from in order to follow God? How does God sustain you in the moments when you want to give up?

4. Jeremiah's ministry can teach just as much about joy as it can about enduring loneliness.

    a. What have you learned from Jeremiah about finding joy in the midst of sorrow?

    b. Where did Jeremiah's joy come from?

    c. Did he still feel pain and agony at the ignorance of Israel? Why did he keep serving the Lord?

    d. Has finding joy in your circumstances and loneliness gotten easier for you? Why?

1. Jeremiah endured his loneliness by himself. How can we work to form deeper connections in the group to make loneliness more bearable?

   a. Take a few minutes to discuss the barriers that could be preventing someone from confiding about loneliness.

2. Our culture and society can sometimes seem to oppose making intimate connections with others. How can we combat against this?

3. Jeremiah was a lonely leader, but he was also fearless in confronting the issue of Israel ignoring God's desire for her to return to Him. Sometimes loneliness is caused not only from standing alone but as the result of confronting an issue.

   a. Have you endured seasons of silence with loved ones because God laid it on your heart to confront an issue?

b. Was the relationship forever changed? Was it lost completely?

c. Did you endure that season of loneliness completely alone, or did you have other relationships that encouraged you? Who were the people you could rely on?

4. Take a few moments and allow group members to talk about a time in their life when loneliness was endured.

a. How did God prove faithful to each of you in your season of loneliness?

b. What lessons can be learned from one another?

c. For those whose loneliness is still ongoing, what encouragement can we offer?

5. Moving forward with the rest of this study, what is a commitment we can make as a group to not only be praying for one another, but also bearing one another's pain during times of loneliness?

a. Pick one person from the group to pray for throughout the duration of this study. Write your prayer below:

DID YOU KNOW?

The name "Jeremiah" means "Yahweh Establishes." God had established Israel and had a plan for it, even though the nation was turning away from Him. God used Jeremiah as a reminder that the Almighty is greater than all circumstances. He established the country and would continue His work regardless of their circumstances.

THE LONELY SON

Genesis 40:1–23

In this lesson we'll look at the life of Joseph who faced problems with God by his side.

OUTLINE

Problems: We can't live with them and it definitely seems we can't live without them. Since problems are inevitable in life, how should we view them? Instead of looking at what problems "cause," looking at what they "contribute" will give us a new perspective.

I. **Problems Provide Us Greater Opportunities**

II. **Problems Promote Our Spiritual Maturity**

III. **Problems Prove Our Integrity**

IV. **Problems Produce a Sense of Dependency**

V. **Problems Prepare Our Hearts for Ministry**

On November 27, 1965, Howard Rutledge parachuted into the hands of the North Vietnamese after his fighter plane exploded under heavy antiaircraft fire. The story of his subsequent seven-year captivity was popularized several years ago in the best-selling book, *In the Presence of Mine Enemies*. In the book, Rutledge tells of being placed inside a six-by-six room at the "Heartbreak Hotel," a notorious prison in Hanoi, with nothing to do for months on end. He lived with rats and filth for years, working to maintain his sanity in a place where he could go for months without ever seeing the sun or sky. It was a terrible ordeal, but through it Rutledge was brought back to God. The Lord had a purpose, even though the circumstances were hard and lonely.

A similar experience is told in Scripture when Joseph was sold into slavery by his brothers. He was just seventeen years old at the time, and for the next thirteen years he would suffer hardships and indignities that were not of his own making. For example, after being sold as a slave to the Egyptian nobleman Potiphar, and after gaining authority over all of Potiphar's affairs, Joseph was falsely accused of sexual assault by Potiphar's wife. Joseph was tossed into a special prison for royal prisoners and taken to the dungeon. It was a lonely, unfair existence for a boy who had done nothing wrong.

Two of the men in prison with him were the king's baker and butler, who checked to make sure none of the food was poisonous. One night those two men had dreams, and they told Joseph about them. The butler's dream, recorded in Genesis 40:9–19, was of a vine that produced grapes, and the butler pressed the grapes and served the wine to Pharaoh. Joseph explained to the butler that his dream meant he would be restored by the king to his original position. The baker's dream was that he had three baskets full of good food resting on his head, but the birds came and snatched the food away. Joseph's interpretation of that dream was that after three days, the baker would be put to death by the king. Both dreams turned out exactly the way Joseph had predicted.

You would think, since Joseph could do something so amazing as interpret dreams, he would be remembered and thanked. But it didn't happen. He remained in his lonely prison, forgotten by the butler whose dream he had explained. That story is told in Scripture not simply to give us some historical detail, but to reveal a truth about God: He allows us to be in tough situations so we might grow. There are advantages to difficulties. As we watch Joseph walk through the various situations of his life, we learn that God has a purpose for each one of us, and in our lives there will sometimes be lonely experiences. There will be problems and difficulties; in the midst of those, God wants to teach us. So let's consider some of the lessons we can learn from the life of Joseph and apply them to our own lives.

Problems Provide Us Greater Opportunities

Problems are often given to us by God to provide us greater opportunities. As God's children, we need to learn how to look for the possibilities in our problems. God's people have always worked this way. An entire section of Scripture, the "prison epistles," was written while Paul was incarcerated in a Roman jail cell. The book of Revelation was written by John while he was exiled on the Isle of Patmos. It was in prison that John Bunyan saw the great allegory that would later become the immortal *Pilgrim's Progress*. Sometimes good things come from bad times.

Joseph learned from his prison experience that he was not forgotten by God. As a matter of fact, God used a relationship formed while Joseph was in prison to accomplish His plan.

I remember hearing Charles Colson say that his lowest times as a believer were far more fulfilling than all his glory days in the White House when he was an unbeliever. During the lonely days of prison, he learned to know God. Sometimes loneliness and difficulties are necessary in our lives because the problems are the means God uses to provide opportunities for us.

Problems Promote Our Spiritual Maturity

The second lesson to learn from the life of Joseph is that problems can make us better if we refuse to let them make us bitter. They promote spiritual maturity. Apart from the Lord Himself, I cannot think of anyone who received more unfair treatment than Joseph. He was repeatedly mistreated. He obeyed his father in going to check on his brothers, and his reward was to be thrown into a pit by those jealous boys and sold to a group of traveling slave traders. He kept his purity and morality while serving in Potiphar's house, and his reward was to be slandered by Potiphar's wife and thrown into a dungeon. While in prison, he faithfully interpreted the dream of a man who vowed to remember him. But as soon as that man returned to his former position, he forgot all about Joseph. It seems that no matter what Joseph did, all he ever got for his good behavior was more trouble and misery.

Despite that, there is not one shred of evidence to suggest that Joseph ever complained. Instead of getting bitter at God, he allowed the Lord to use the experiences of his life to make him a better person. Joseph probably had a soft life as a child. While his brothers were out working, he was walking around in his special coat. While the other boys were toiling in the fields, Joseph was living like a young prince. So if God were to use Joseph, He would have to toughen him up. The task ahead required a strong man. The Lord would have to make him ready to be prime minister of Egypt during a worldwide famine. Psalm 105:17–18 reads, "He sent a man before them—Joseph—*who* was sold as a slave. They hurt his feet with fetters, he was laid in irons." So Joseph was apparently chained up while in that dungeon, but in putting on those iron chains, iron also entered his soul. When Joseph came out of that prison, he was a man of great wisdom, courage, and determination. He acted like a leader. When he ascended to a high place in the government of Egypt, he carried the nation through a terrible famine without any signs of revolt. Joseph was prepared for the hardship of that famine because he had been hardened by his experience in prison.

God wants to develop some "iron saints" in our own day, and the only way that iron can ever enter our souls is if God allows us to experience suffering. We become stronger people by going through tough times. As the writer to the Hebrews put it, "No chastening seems to be joyful for the present, but painful; nevertheless, afterward it yields the peaceable fruit of righteousness to those who have been trained by it" (12:11). This concept of becoming strong through hard times is being assaulted today by success and prosperity preachers. They make the argument that you cannot be sick and cannot fail if you trust God. But the New Testament is filled with stories of those who got sick, were beaten, went through hard times, and became stronger because of their difficulties. The Bible doesn't promise us that we will go from cradle to grave without problems. Problems are sometimes God's gift to help make us strong. To get out of the problem may be to abort God's process of growth. For example, if Joseph's brother Reuben had made good on his intention to help Joseph escape from the pit, his brother would have missed the entire ministry God had planned. If Potiphar had rejected the accusations of his wife, though he must have had serious doubts about them, Joseph would never have been prepared for greatness.

Problems are the avenues God uses to cause our growth so we can face the challenges. Problems promote our maturity.

PROBLEMS PROVE OUR INTEGRITY

If our character is genuine, it is not altered by circumstances. Joseph was a man of great character, so he was willing to be God's man no matter what circumstances he was in.

Character is often confused with reputation, but there is a vast difference. Reputation is what others think we are; character is what we really are. Reputation is what men think we are; character is what God knows we are. Reputation is what is chiseled in our tombstone; character is what the angels say about us before God.

Character never changes, even when circumstances change. Problems prove our integrity. Once in a while I will hear people say, "But my situation made me this way!" No, the situation doesn't make us do anything, it simply reveals who we are. When we face the difficulties of life, it is a wonderful opportunity for God to use us to demonstrate the reality and integrity of our character in front of others.

PROBLEMS PRODUCE A SENSE OF DEPENDENCY

In Genesis 39:20–21 we read,

Then Joseph's master took him and put him into the prison, a place where the king's prisoners *were* confined. And he was there in the prison. But the LORD was with Joseph and showed him mercy, and He gave him favor in the sight of the keeper of the prison.

Everywhere Joseph went, God went with him. The only thing that can separate you from God is sin, not circumstance. As long as we keep our lives pure, He will go before us and be with us. But sin separates us from God. It breaks the fellowship; so whatever your problems might be, we need to make sure we are righteous before the Lord. Whether we are in a pit or a palace, God will go with us.

While he was in prison, Joseph found out how much the Lord loved him. Many times in my life I've heard people tell me, "Pastor, I always knew God loved me, but I've never known the fellowship that I have known in these hard times. God has been with me." Problems come into our lives to show us how dependent we are upon the Lord. Our society pushes self-sufficiency; if we're not careful, we may think we don't need the Lord quite as much as we used to. But just when we start thinking that way, God will put us into prison for a while so we can be reminded how dependent we are on Him. Problems produce a sense of dependency on the Lord.

PROBLEMS PREPARE OUR HEARTS FOR MINISTRY

In Genesis 40:6–7 are some amazing words: "And Joseph came in to them in the morning and looked at them, and saw that they *were* sad. So he asked Pharaoh's officers who *were* with him in the custody of his lord's house, saying, 'Why do you look *so* sad today?'" What makes this so amazing is that Joseph, a lonely prisoner unjustly put into a dungeon, notices somebody else's attitude. Here is a guy who had every right to be wrapped up in self-pity, wondering why God allowed such sorry circumstances, but instead he is serving others. He is sensitive, loving, and sympathetic. He notices their sad faces, initiates the conversation, and ministers to the prisoners. There is no ministry to the suffering like that offered by another sufferer.

Paul told the Corinthians that we comfort others with the comfort with which we ourselves have been comforted. When we are put into difficult circumstances in life, we are made sensitive to others around us who have similar problems. When my family was going through a difficult time, I was called and encouraged by two men who were experiencing very hard times. Suffering seems to bring out a heart for ministry. It's hard to reach out to others if we ourselves have never suffered. Sometimes it is just necessary to say, "I know how you feel." Sometimes God allows us to experience troubles to get us ready to help someone else. Not long after Donna had a miscarriage, I had to do my first funeral—for a couple who had just lost a baby. I knew a little bit about what they felt. Joseph, through his prison experience, became a servant of everyone. God broke his heart while in prison so that he was able to serve others.

Problems have advantages. They provide us with greater opportunities if we will only look for the possibilities in our problems. They promote spiritual maturity if we let them make us better instead of bitter. They prove our integrity because character is not a factor of circumstance. They produce a sense of dependency on the presence of the Lord and His power. And they prepare our heart for ministry so that in the midst of our sufferings, we can serve others.

Why did God put Howard Rutledge, the American fighter pilot, into a Viet Cong prison? To prepare him for something greater.

Rutledge had become disinterested in the Christian faith, but his imprisonment brought him back to the Lord. It helped him to remember the importance of the Bible, the blessing of his family, and the necessity of going to church. The Lord puts people in prison so they can learn and grow. I don't like troubles, and my natural desire is to run from them, but I know God wants to use them to shape me. Too often we want the crown without the cross, the resurrection without the death, and the gain without the pain. God will not allow it. Troubles will come into our personal lives, our families, our churches, but God can take these problems and make us better—if we cooperate with Him. Don't run from the pressures God wants to use to make you His perfect example of Christlikeness.

1. How is Joseph's story an example of loneliness?

   a. Would it have been easy for him to be bitter? What did he do instead of allowing bitterness to take root in his heart?

   b. What can be said about the power of forgiveness in a lonely situation?

   c. When your thoughts rage and emotions cause turmoil in your heart, what Scripture can you rely on to remind you that God is your companion and comfort in the midst of any lonely season?

2. As you read in this lesson, the apostle Paul wrote a good portion of the New Testament while in prison. Read Philippians 1.

   a. How does Paul's time in prison reflect a similar message to that of Joseph's time in prison?

   b. God redeemed Paul's and Joseph's time in prison to fit His purpose and plan. How can you be encouraged that your suffering is part of a greater plan?

c. What can you say was Paul's greatest comfort during his suffering? What was Joseph's greatest comfort?

3. What can be said about the value of unity and fellowship in times of loneliness?

   a. What do you think Joseph and Paul learned from the occasional reality of having no one who could relate to their suffering?

   b. What did both men have to train themselves to remember in the midst of their loneliness?

4. Take a few moments to think about your own life. Looking back, was there a season of loneliness that God used for His purpose?

   a. What is one thing God taught you about Himself using that time of suffering?

   b. How can you use what you've learned to minister to others in similar seasons?

1. Joseph, as a young man, lived a life of favor before being sold into slavery by his brothers. As a group, as each feels led, share about the life you led before your suffering and loneliness appeared.

   a. Could you see yourself accomplishing what God has accomplished through you if He hadn't allowed you to suffer?

2. We read in this lesson that God allows suffering in our lives so we may become stronger for the plans He has for us.

   a. Has there ever been a time when we doubted that our pain would bring a good result?

   b. How do we learn to trust God in the midst of our loneliness?

c. What Scriptures can reassure us of God's faithfulness in the plans He has for us, even in suffering and pain brought on by loneliness?

3. Suffering allows us to be prepared to minister to others. How have we been ministering to others? How have you been the one to receive the ministry of another?

   a. What does fellowship through suffering say about God's plan for unity?

   b. How could Joseph have benefited from fellowship? Would he have possibly suffered from fellowship? Would he have learned how to fully rely on God's faithfulness? Why or why not?

4. What can we learn from Joseph's ability to allow God to harden his heart?

a. How can this encourage us as we learn to let God form iron in our own hearts?

b. What can God possibly accomplish through us when we have iron helping us to stand under the pain of loneliness?

5. How can the group minister to its members who may be suffering at this very moment?

DID YOU KNOW?

The coat of many colors that Jacob gave to Joseph wasn't actually multicolored, but white with colored decoration or trim. The words used to describe it literally mean a long dress robe, worn by a prince or lord who didn't work in the fields. It must have effectively separated Joseph from his brothers!

THE LONELY SOLDIER

2 Timothy 4:9–22

In this lesson we'll examine how Paul handled disappointment.

OUTLINE

Everybody gets disappointed at some time, but those in ministry are particularly susceptible to it. The apostle Paul, while in prison in Rome, wrote to Timothy and revealed his feelings, offering ideas for overcoming disappointment.

I. The Disappointments in Paul's Life
  A. His Disappointment That Comes With Discomfort
  B. His Disappointment Due to Detachment From Friends
  C. His Disappointment From Defection
  D. His Disappointment of Difficulty
  E. His Disappointment of Desertion

II. Dealing With Disappointment in Our Lives
  A. Physical Encouragements
  B. Personal Encouragements
  C. Mental Encouragements
  D. Spiritual Encouragements

For those who give themselves to a life of faith, to living a holy life for God, and to being committed to the task of evangelism, there is often a sense of loneliness which has to be endured. Pastors and missionaries are particularly susceptible to loneliness, for there is a price to pay in serving the Lord. Sometimes it is the shortage of cash or the lack of material things or even the inability to provide a proper education for your children. But the biggest cost of serving God is often loneliness. As one missionary put it to me, "There is never anyone there to applaud you, no social whirlwind that you can fit into, and no opportunity to be a part of people in the normal courses of life." To be a servant of the Lord is to be a breed apart. Anyone who puts his hand to the plow knows the crushing load of responsibility that comes with it.

I don't think anyone fully considers that cost at the time of commitment. We probably all believe that God will take care of things, and He does in the end. But the pressures can still bring moments of loneliness when we feel fragile and helpless, even though we are a servant of the King. I once chatted with a female missionary who said the worst part of her work was never getting close to anyone back home. People would pray for her, but they didn't really know her. While on deputation, she couldn't really be herself because no church is interested in a missionary with problems. Too many Christians assume that a life of faith has no human frailties. But most Christian leaders don't want to be viewed as superhuman. They want to be accepted as people, not performers. They want to be friends, not just frontier warriors.

Every servant of God, whether a missionary, pastor, or someone toiling for a Christian ministry, has experienced this sort of discouragement and disappointment. It just seems to come with the territory. Certainly the apostle Paul understood it; for in his last letter to Timothy, he concluded by telling about some of the disappointments in his life.

The Disappointments in Paul's Life

His Disappointment That Comes With Discomfort

Paul, who was being held in the infamous Mamertine Prison, was exposed to the chill and damp of his cell. It reeked with pestilence, vividly reminding him of the generations of criminals who had sat before him in that very place. Paul undoubtedly knew there would be no escape from his cell apart from death. He'd had a preliminary audience with Caesar and had done well, but it was certainly a matter of time before his fate was decided. And Paul no doubt knew what the decision would be. The feeling of the public toward the apostle was hostility, and Christians were considered traitors against Rome at that time for proposing the treasonous idea of fealty to another King.

The dark cloud that hung over Paul is summarized in his words to Timothy: "For I am already being poured out as a drink offering, and the time of my departure is at hand. I have fought the good fight, I have finished the race, I have kept the faith" (2 Timothy 4:6–7). Paul knew he was about to be sentenced to death. Tradition tells us that he was beheaded on Ostian Way, the very day Peter was crucified upside down on a cross at the command of Nero.

The discomfort Paul felt certainly lent itself to disappointment. He was in a miserable situation physically. He was cold, tired, and locked in a dark, damp cell. C. S. Lewis has noted that "our bodies and souls live so close together that they catch each other's diseases," so when we are physically down, it is hard to be spiritually up. The physical plight of Paul made it extremely tough for him to be comfortable, and his discomfort brought with it disappointment.

His Disappointment Due to Detachment From Friends

I am convinced that the greatest pain Paul felt was not physical, but spiritual. He was anguished in his soul as he wrote to Timothy, for "all those in Asia have turned away from me, among whom are Phygellus and Hermogenes" (2 Timothy 1:15). Some of those who had ministered side by side with Paul had defected from the Church. "Demas has forsaken me, having loved this present world, and has departed for Thessalonica" (4:10). Not only had some of his best friends left the faith, others close to him had departed for other lands: "Crescens [has left] for Galatia, Titus for Dalmatia . . . . Tychicus I have sent to Ephesus" (4:10, 12). His friend Erastus had been left in Corinth, Tromphimus had become sick and remained in Miletus, and at his hearing, "no one stood with me, but all forsook me" (verse 16). Not only that, but "Alexander the coppersmith did me much harm" (verse 14). There is an aching loneliness in the words of Paul when he writes, "Only Luke is with me" (verse 11). Sending greetings to friends far away, Paul asks his friend, "Do your utmost to come before winter" (verse 21). He was detached from his friends during a time of crisis, making him feel lonely.

Earlier in this epistle, Paul had instructed Timothy to be bold. In those passages you get a feel for the steel in Paul's soul. But at the end of the letter, you also get a glimpse of Paul's humanity, his flesh and blood. Here is a man who gets tired and lonely and disappointed, just like all the rest of us. Being separated from friends can do that to you.

His Disappointment From Defection

Not only have Paul's friends left him, but one man is singled out for his particular failings. Demas defected from Paul and fled to the city of Thessalonica. His desertion was particularly painful to Paul, for Demas was one of his closest associates. In fact, the only other place where Demas' name appears in Scripture is in conjunction with Luke (Colossians 4:14), the faithful friend who remained with Paul. His close friend Demas had left, according to Paul, "having loved this present world" (2 Timothy 4:10). What a sad commentary on the man.

There is an interesting contrast in the text of Paul's letter. In chapter 4, verse 8, Paul is talking about those who love the appearing of Christ, but in verse 10 he is describing one who loves this world. That's a reminder to us that we cannot choose both. We will stand with God or we will stand with the world, and Demas had made his choice. He refused to stand with his friend Paul in his love for the Lord, choosing instead to embrace the world. Perhaps he defected out of cowardice since the government at that time was making it very hard on Christians. Many Christians have done that over time, exclaiming, "That's it! It's not worth it. I'm quitting." Then they've walked away from the cause. It's a hard thing to watch, and it leaves friends feeling hurt and alone.

It sometimes seems that not a week goes by that I don't hear of someone I know who has defected from the faith, either spiritually or morally. I understand how Paul felt since I have counted some of those defectors as friends and fellow laborers in the Lord. When Paul was in his moment of need, facing the possibility of death, his trusted aide defected. What tremendous pain the apostle must have felt.

His Disappointment of Difficulty

In verses 14 and 15, Paul mentions Alexander the coppersmith who "did me much harm. May the Lord repay him according to his works." Paul goes on to warn Timothy, "You also must beware of him, for he has greatly resisted our words." We don't know anything about this character, except for the fact that he caused Paul great harm.

The word translated as "harm" literally means to be an informer, and many believe Alexander was the man who caused Paul to be arrested and imprisoned.

But Alexander was more than an informer, for he opposed Paul in many ways. He stood up and fought against the Gospel. He was an enemy of Paul and an enemy of Jesus Christ. We cannot take a stand for the Lord and not make enemies. Of course, Paul found that to be true on a number of occasions. Throughout his ministry he was confronted with people who opposed him and made life hard for him. Some may talk about moving through difficulties victoriously, but I've found that it's hard to face problems with churches and personal acquaintances. It doesn't feel good, and it's going to be hard no matter what.

A pastor, or anyone, can get stuck on an Alexander. Everybody else may be encouraging and positive, but there in the back at every service is Alexander, trying to wreck things for you. It gets really discouraging. Early in my ministry, we had a man like that, and I spent way too much time dwelling on him. Then one day I absentmindedly started flipping through the church directory and was reminded of the many godly, supportive families we had in the church. I realized Satan wanted to use that Alexander to discourage me. I got a new perspective on my work for God. It's easy to see why Paul was experiencing so much disappointment with men like Alexander trying to make things hard for him.

His Disappointment of Desertion

At Paul's first defense, when he really needed some character witnesses and a few guys to offer him moral support, there was nobody. No one showed up. Now Roman law would not have permitted Paul to employ an advocate or call character witnesses, but the thought of having some supportive friends in attendance would have cheered him. Imagine his disappointment when no one was brave enough to stand with him. We know from history that many trumped-up charges were made against the Early Church leaders. But for this man to have to stand without anyone else to cheer him must have deeply wounded Paul.

Have you ever been in a crisis and unable to find anyone to help you? That's how Paul felt. It's one thing to be lonely while facing the routine tasks of life, but to be left alone when facing a life-and-death crisis must have put an awfully heavy load on Paul. It's the same feeling Jesus must have had when His closest followers deserted Him in the Garden of Gethsemane.

DEALING WITH DISAPPOINTMENT IN OUR LIVES

I don't want you to think that Paul was a bitter or disappointed man because he was not. The rest of his letter reveals a man with a solid faith in Christ who trusted in the leading of God. As a matter of fact, the seeds of a solution are found planted in the very problem. As you read through that last chapter of 2 Timothy, you'll find some great insights for dealing with disappointment in your own life.

Physical Encouragements

First, remember that there are sometimes physical encouragements. For example, Paul was kept in a cold cell, but he wrote and asked Timothy to bring his coat. That's a reminder that needs can sometimes be met very simply. It also reminds us that each of us can minister to others in big ways by doing some very small things. After all, Paul didn't want someone to put him on the prayer list so much as he wanted somebody to say an encouraging word and maybe bring a warm jacket to his cell. Christians often elevate a physical need into a spiritual realm, and the problem is that the need never gets met. If Paul needs a coat, somebody should bring him a coat and offer some physical encouragement to him.

Personal Encouragements

Not only are there physical encouragements, there are also personal encouragements. In verse 11, Paul asks Timothy to bring Mark with him, noting that "he is useful to me for ministry." Mark had been a deserter on Paul's first missionary journey, and had caused a division between Paul and his first partner, Barnabas. But at the end of his life, Paul wanted his personal friendship with Mark restored. More than that, Paul wanted to see his friend Timothy face-to-face. "Be diligent to come to me quickly," he tells his young protégé (verse 9). Paul needed the same sort of friendship we all need. Occasionally we meet people who claim they don't need friends, that they can get by with "just Jesus and me." But I'm not sure I believe them. I couldn't survive ministry without somebody else to share my joy and pain. As wonderful and exciting as the presence of the Lord is, it isn't intended as a total substitute for human friendship.

People in ministry need friends, and often need one special friend. I have someone like that who has been there for me when things have been great and when things have been hard. When I need somebody, all I have to do is pick up the phone and tell him what's on my heart. Everybody needs that. Paul had it in Timothy.

Mental Encouragements

There are also mental encouragements. Paul asked Timothy to bring his books and parchments to him so that he could occupy his mind while he sat in his cell. I've often found that, aside from the Bible, there isn't anything that can speak to a particular need better than a book which offers good advice on that particular problem. I think people watch television because it doesn't require anything from their brain, but a good book can fill your mind and have a therapeutic value to your life, ministering to you mentally.

Spiritual Encouragements

Finally, there are spiritual encouragements. Paul knew that "the Lord stood with me" when he sat in court (verse 17). He could sense God's presence, and there are times that sensing His presence is what we need most. When we're cold, we need a coat. When we're lonely we need a friend. When we're bored, we need something to ponder. And when we feel that all those human props have been taken away, we need to sense the presence of God in our lives. It is that presence which keeps minds from bending in prison cells, which keeps the heat from melting a body in the jungle, and which keeps God's servants preaching faithfully though all manner of opposition rise against them. It is the presence of Christ which can keep us going when nothing else is there. We see Paul waiting for death, disappointed at his circumstances, but also triumphant, knowing that he is about to meet his Lord who will set him free from the vale of tears and make him more than a conqueror in a world set on his destruction.

1. The apostle Paul is a reminder that being a leader can be difficult. What are some reasons a leader, the one who seemingly has everything figured out, may suffer from disappointment?

   a. Who are your leaders? Why do you look up to them?

   b. Do you ever find yourself thinking they have everything figured out? If so, how can you remind yourself that they have struggles just like you?

   c. How can you be an encouragement to them this week?

2. Read 2 Timothy 4:6-22.

   a. What is the state of Paul's heart?

b. How can you relate to him?

c. Have you ever felt abandoned or betrayed by close friends or family? Were those relationships ever restored? What did you have to do to forgive them?

3. Sometimes loneliness is a result of actions. What was Paul's loneliness from?

a. How does this offer reassurance that sometimes loneliness is not a result of sin?

b. Loneliness and the resultant suffering can bring out the weaknesses in you and others, causing relationships to be lost. What relationships have you lost?

c. How did you cope with the disappointment brought on by feeling alone, abandoned?

d. Have you left someone alone in their suffering? If so, how can you seek their forgiveness?

4. Examine your relationships.

   a. Who has stuck with you? Who hasn't?

   b. Looking back, are you grateful those relationships were tested?

   c. Who are the ones you know you can rely on for encouragement when life goes sideways?

   d. How can the testing of your relationships not only make you stronger, but show the strength you already have?

1. As a group, take a few moments to allow for members to share a season when they felt abandoned by someone they needed, or had relied on in the past.

   a. What lessons can be learned from these personal stories?

   b. Discuss a few ways you can form stronger bonds within the group to encourage one another.

   c. How can we encourage the leader this week?

2. How can we allow our relationships in every area of our life to be strengthened through our suffering rather than weakened?

   a. What can loneliness teach us about our relationships with others? Our relationship with Christ?

b. If our loneliness isn't brought on by being called to stand alone (as we saw with Jeremiah), how can we make sure those around us will "stick closer than a brother"? (Proverbs 18:24)

c. What are some reasons we might feel the need to withhold our suffering, loneliness, and disappointment from those we love?

d. Would this decision ever help us? Or would it ultimately hurt us in the end?

3. Sometimes the strengths and weaknesses of our relationships make us question our individual strengths and weaknesses. Why is it important to remember that our relationships are meant to be a source of encouragement?

4. Within the group, give each person a few minutes to share an area in their life where they need encouragement.

a. How can we be a physical encouragement to one another?

b. How can we be a personal encouragement to one another?

c. How can we be a mental encouragement to one another?

d. How can we be a spiritual encouragement to one another?

Constructed in 7 B.C., the Mamertine Prison was used as a place of detention for criminals who were awaiting execution. Some prisoners, however, died from starvation in the cramped, miserable quarters. The two-celled building is located near the Forum in Rome, Italy. Originally, the only access into the lower cell was by rope through a hole in the ground. Today, visitors can use a narrow flight of stairs to see the place where tradition dictates that both Peter and Paul spent time before their deaths.

THE LONELY SUFFERER

Psalm 116

*In this lesson we'll take a look at the depression
David experienced and how he worked through it.*

OUTLINE

Nobody likes having to suffer, though God sometimes allows suffering. The psalmist David went through some very hard times, and the lessons he learned from them can be applied to all of our lives.

I. **The Characteristics of Sickness**
    A. Discomfort
    B. Despair
    C. Depression
    D. Dependence
    E. Despondence
    F. Dread

II. **The Cries of Sickness**
    A. God Heard
    B. God Helped
    C. God Healed

III. **The Lessons of Sickness**
    A. "I Will Remember My Promise to Him"
    B. "I Will Render My Love to Him"
    C. "I Will Return My Thanks to Him"
    D. "I Will Receive His Great Salvation"

When you read Psalm 116, you get a feeling for the difficult times David went through as king of Israel. One of the difficulties in reading the psalms is trying to figure out when they were written so we can tie them to events in the author's life. Frankly I don't know when it was written or where David was at the time. It's possible the psalm is simply a presentation of David's own spiritual renewal. But it is couched in words of physical suffering and hurt, and it provides a wonderful opportunity to listen to the poetic mind of the great Old Testament singer as he describes the emotions he went through in one difficult and lonely time of his life.

> I love the LORD, because He has heard
> My voice *and* my supplications.
> Because He has inclined His ear to me,
> Therefore I will call *upon Him* as long as I live.
> The pains of death surrounded me,
> And the pangs of Sheol laid hold of me;
> I found trouble and sorrow.
> Then I called upon the name of the LORD:
> "O LORD, I implore You, deliver my soul!"
> Gracious *is* the LORD, and righteous;
> Yes, our God *is* merciful,
> The LORD preserves the simple;
> I was brought low, and He saved me.
> Return to your rest, O my soul,
> For the LORD has dealt bountifully with you.
> For you have delivered my soul from death,
> My eyes from tears,
> *And* my feet from falling.
> I will walk before the LORD
> In the land of the living.
> I believed, therefore I spoke,
> "I am greatly afflicted."
> I said in my haste,
> "All men *are* liars."
> What shall I render to the LORD
> *For* all His benefits toward me?
> I will take up the cup of salvation,
> And call upon the name of the LORD.
> I will pay my vows to the LORD
> Now in the presence of all His people.
> Precious in the sight of the LORD

Is the death of His saints.
O LORD, truly I *am* Your servant;
I *am* your servant, the son of Your maidservant;
You have loosed my bonds.
I will offer to You the sacrifice of thanksgiving,
And will call upon the name of the LORD.
I will pay my vows to the LORD
Now in the presence of all His people,
In the courts of the LORD'S house,
In the midst of you, O Jerusalem.
Praise the LORD!

THE CHARACTERISTICS OF SICKNESS
Discomfort
The first thing that we see in that poem is the various characteristics that go along with sickness. For example, David describes his discomfort. He actually uses the term "pain" to describe what he is going through. It makes me think of C. S. Lewis who said that "God whispers to us in our pleasures, speaks in our conscience, but shouts in our pains: it is His megaphone to arouse a deaf world."

Despair
A second characteristic of sickness is despair. David spoke of the sorrow he felt in terms of death. Sickness and suffering can do that to us, turning our thoughts toward the end of life and filling us with sorrow.

Depression
Closely related to despair is depression, something we all experience at times. David wrote about tears filling his eyes, and much of his psalm has a depressed quality to it. Whatever he was going through, the king was clearly depressed. His circumstances had brought him down. Serious illness often brings on depression. A friend of mine who spent a long time in bed battling a persistent physical illness told me that his fight with depression was almost worse than his fight with the actual disease. For in depression he could only imagine the worst, and though he was normally a strong, happy person, he realized he was helpless against the power of that disease.

Dependence
David goes on to say that there came a sort of dependence in his situation. In verse 8, he writes of his feet being kept from falling—not something he did for himself, but something for which he had to depend on another. I don't think there is anything more difficult

about a hospital stay than to recognize that you are no longer in charge of yourself. You leave your dignity outside when you enter the hospital doors. I used to live in dread of going to the hospital when I pastored in Fort Wayne, for almost all of our church college group was made up of students in the nursing school. And I just knew I'd be left in the hands of young people in our church who would see their pastor without any dignity. Someone has said that we spend all our lives learning how to clothe ourselves for the sake of modesty, only to have it unravel in the mockery of a hospital smock. The one thing you can be sure of is that no matter where you sit down, it's cold! There is something undignified about being sick and in the hospital, totally dependent upon others.

Despondence

David goes on to say that another characteristic of sickness is despondence. He cried out to God about his situation. He even accused others of lying to him, as if the world had all turned against him in some crazy sort of conspiracy. I can almost hear him wail, "Why has God done this to me? Would somebody please explain?" If you've talked to people who have experienced a serious illness, you know that many of them struggle with a sense of guilt. They've heard some preacher tell them that people get sick due to their sin, and they fear in the back of their mind that they've slipped up somewhere. But God allows sickness for a variety of reasons, including to get our attention and to make us slow down and learn dependence on Him. The God we serve is not a God who spends His time retaliating for past sins, particularly confessed and forgiven sins. One time I had a young woman say to me, "I know God forgives me, but I just can't forgive myself." To that I answered, "Oh, so your own standards are higher than God's?" All of a sudden, a light went on in her head. She realized that if God had forgiven her sin, she had been cleared by the highest authority possible. We don't have to feel guilty and despondent over our sickness; God is using it to get our attention and to shape us in some way.

Dread

One last characteristic of sickness that David mentions is dread. Three times he talks about death, concluding in verse 15 by saying, "Precious . . . is the death of His saints." There is an earnestness to the prayers of the dying. Those closest to seeing Him face-to-face have an intensity to their prayers that the rest of us often lack. In his psalm, David has captured the characteristics of sickness quite well. But he doesn't just describe the situation, he also tells what he did in the midst of it.

THE CRIES OF SICKNESS
God Heard

There are three truths that we can take from this psalm. The first is that when I cry, God hears me. In verses 1 and 2, David says exactly that: "I love the LORD, because He has heard my voice." My mental picture is that of the Father leaning down to hear the cry of His hurting child. When we cry, God hears us. He knows what we are going through.

God Helped

Second, David makes clear that when we cry, God helps us. In verse 7 we read, "Return to your rest, O my soul, for the LORD has dealt bountifully with you." In other words, God not only heard, He also helped. He gave me what I needed, though it may not have been exactly what I asked for. He knows when we need help, and He is there to help us.

God Healed

Third, David goes on to tell us that when we cry, God heals us. The psalm says that God healed David, protected him, and loosed his bonds. God can choose to heal us, though He may choose not to. I was at a conference a few years ago, and I had the opportunity to hear Tony Campolo speak. When he was asked about the problems with the modern "healing" movement, he responded by saying that many Christians have been led astray by false teaching. It is not God's will for everyone to be healed, as anyone who has read the New Testament should know. Many times the Lord walked into a situation where there were many sick and hurting, and He chose to heal some. Others He left in their condition. It is not God's will that we shall all be healed here on earth. Ultimately, of course, everyone will be healed. A day is coming when the Lord will take us home, and we shall be with Him, and all the diseases of our physical body will go away. We will all be healed and whole. Some may be healed here on earth, but someday all will be healed in heaven. It is that sort of confidence that David has when he exults in the power of the Lord. That's why he can say that the death of a saint is precious to God— that saint is suddenly brought into wholeness of body and spirit.

THE LESSONS OF SICKNESS

In verse 12, David asks an excellent question: "What shall I render to the LORD *for* all His benefits toward me?" What can we learn from our experiences? What should my response be to God for all that I've endured? That is a question we rarely ask, so obsessed are we with getting well. But David asks it, and he comes up with at least four answers, all introduced by the little phrase, "I will."

"I Will Remember My Promise to Him"

David had made a vow to God; after he is through the experience, he remembers to keep his vow. Too many Christians, lying in a sickbed somewhere, have made vows to God regarding their time and money if only they will get well, then forgotten all about the vow as soon as their health returns. If we are sick and offer a vow to the Lord, it is our responsibility to remember and keep that vow. To break it is to lie to God.

"I Will Render My Love to Him"

It's interesting that the concept of love is woven throughout a poem about sickness. David tells us that he loves God, and he will continue to love God, even though things aren't going his way right now. It's easy to love God when we are healthy and prosperous, but God wants us to love and trust Him even when our health and wealth have been taken away. He is God over all circumstances, and He deserves our love and devotion regardless of circumstance.

"I Will Return My Thanks to Him"

Though it must have been hard to be thankful in the midst of suffering, David knew he owed everything to God. He chose to be thankful, though he didn't like his circumstance. I heard about a little girl who had to go through a painful operation. The doctor told her, "This will hurt, but you have my permission to cry or scream." Instead the girl said, "If it's all right with you, I'd rather sing." And sing she did. Sometimes we have to thank God for His plan and His love, even though we can't see it at the moment.

"I Will Receive His Great Salvation"

In verse 13, David speaks of taking up the cup of salvation. Sometimes God allows someone to be physically ill, perhaps even life-threateningly ill, in order for them to consider their need for eternal life. When sickness comes, we remember that even though our life might be in danger, we owe our very life to the Lord. If we are to die on this earth, we know that we'll be with Him in eternity.

A young lady in our church in the Midwest, Susan Leonard Johnson, developed terminal cancer. She had been in a Bible study with several of the women of the church; after her death, those ladies gave me a copy of a poem Susan wrote which described her journey with the Lord. Though it was a painful time of suffering, the poem reveals where that young lady placed her faith:

When I was just a child of five, and learned about my Lord,
I never shouted, "Prove it!" and I never felt ignored.
My hands were always folded in innocent belief.
It was easy to be humble, Him above and me beneath.
There was no cause to question or to complicate this view,
And I'd often hear Him whisper, "Oh, my child, I love you, too."
When I was one-and-twenty and learned about my world,
How wise I'd grown. I'd outgrown God. My future was unfurled.
Lord, You know me well, so I won't pray.
And I don't need You anyway.
How soon I'm one-and-thirty. Why is life such a bore?
I'm falling short in everything, and everything's a chore.
I have so much, I've done so much, this emptiness is wrong.
"There is no God," my logic cries, "I knew it all along.
Lord, I doubt, and cannot pray one whit.
I will not be a hypocrite!"
Now I'm four-and-thirty, and the void is magnified.
I do not understand it all, how desperately I've tried!
Disease has made its debut, and I scream that it's unfair.
I'm only given one more year, and I sink in sheer despair.
My girls are small, and I'm so young. They say there is no hope.
The fear is all-consuming. Please, someone, help me cope!
"Lord, could that be You that knocks again?
Forgive me, Lord, Oh, please come in."
Gathering up my burdens, He said this about my strife:
"You've been dead for over thirty years, and now I'll show
you life."
Today I'm five-and-thirty, what a blessed year it's been!
The fear was changed to utter peace, there's happiness again.
What time unfolds, I do not know, but that's not my concern.
Once again, by grace I humbly trust. A precious lesson learned.
"Lord, I give all myself to You."
"Oh, My child, I love you, too!"

Susan Leonard Johnson was dead for 34 years. Then she got cancer and came alive! If you had the perspective of eternity, what would you choose?

1. David suffered greatly during his lifetime. How is his suffering an encouragement for you?

   a. What lessons did God teach him?

   b. What was the reason behind those frequent seasons of pain?

   c. How did David allow his relationship with Christ to be strengthened through these seasons?

   d. Do you think David suffered for his sins? Or do you think it was God carrying out a greater plan for his life? Why?

   e. What other psalms has David written on the topic of suffering and loneliness? What is a common theme that restored his joy, even in the midst of trials?

2. When God allows, or has allowed, suffering and pain to take place in your life, what is the takeaway?

   a. If you are on the other side of your season of loneliness, what do you think was the reason(s) for it?

b. What lessons did you learn from being completely dependent on God for your comfort?

c. What areas of your life seemed blurry before your season of pain? What clarity was given to you after the season had passed?

d. How did your faith grow through that time?

3. Translate David's life into your modern life. Do you know anyone who has had struggles similar to those David endured?

a. Have you suffered as David did? Or do you feel you are suffering right now? What truths can you hold onto that will encourage you in this season?

b. What are some ways you can use your season of suffering to encourage others in their own seasons of loneliness and pain?

c. Write down the name of someone you think may be suffering right now, and commit to pray for them this week.

1. Read Psalm 138.

   a. Comparing this psalm to Psalm 116, how does it show David's ongoing maturity and dependence on God?

   b. How does God draw David back into communion and fellowship?

   c. Does dependence upon God mean we will never suffer? Or perhaps our suffering will vanish when we come into fellowship with Him? Why or why not?

2. In this lesson, we read about sickness and its characteristics. What sicknesses are we currently suffering through?

a. Do we progress through each listed characteristic? Or do we go through a back-and-forth battle with all of them?

b. What is something David tells us to remember or hold onto in our battles with suffering?

c. How is God using each listed characteristic to strengthen and bring us into fellowship with Him? What evidence do we see of this?

3. The New Testament is filled with stories of people who had to endure seasons of suffering, even people who followed Jesus and led others to Him. How can their suffering be an encouragement rather than a discouragement to us as we suffer?

a. The apostle Paul and others in the New Testament endured suffering and loneliness after begging to be free of the burden. What was God's purpose in allowing their suffering to persist?

b. Did they endure their suffering alone? Who did they have to comfort and encourage them?

c. How can we encourage one another and bear the burdens that we can't always handle on our own?

DID YOU KNOW?

Paul suffered from extremely poor eyesight, though that was not necessarily the "thorn in the flesh" he speaks of in 2 Corinthians. Notice that in Galatians 6:11 Paul, who normally had a scribe write his dictated letters, speaks of trying to write with his own hand. His eyesight made it difficult. Imagine how much tougher that must have made Paul's travels and ministry.

THE LONELY SPOUSE

Ephesians 5:25

*In this lesson we'll look at God's instructions
to Christian husbands and wives.*

OUTLINE

Our culture doesn't really understand what love is all about. We
get our ideas of marital love from movies, but the Bible says
our love for one another should be like the love Jesus has
for the Church.

I. **Consequences for the Unloved Spouse**
    A. Get a Job
    B. Join a Militant Women's Group
    C. Become Depressed
    D. Infidelity
    E. Escape Through Drugs and Alcohol
    F. Desertion

II. **Characteristics of Christ's Love**
    A. His Love Is Realistic
    B. His Love Is Sacrificial
    C. His Love Is Purposeful
    D. His Love Is Willing
    E. His Love Is Absolute

Some months ago a very lonely woman wrote to her counselor, telling about her relationship with her husband. They had been deeply in love when they got married, but things began to change after a few short years. They needed money, so her husband began working longer hours. That not only kept them apart, it fatigued him to the point where he was almost uncommunicative in the few moments they had together each evening. She would have much to tell him about, but he was too tired to reply. Then he started filling his extra time with business meetings and golf games, leaving his wife with only three small children to talk to. Eventually they drifted apart. He never took her on dates, never offered a romantic gift or note, and even forgot their last anniversary. There was no closeness or warmth in their relationship, and that poor wife never felt so lonely.

Sadly, that same description can be repeated countless times for women in our modern world. Perhaps as many as ninety percent of divorces are due to loneliness from living together but feeling separated. When a man neglects his wife and family, the result is loneliness for everyone involved.

CONSEQUENCES FOR THE UNLOVED SPOUSE

The results of a man who neglects his wife and family and creates lonely feelings can't all be charted, but here are a few we can trace in this study.

Get a Job

Many women respond to the loneliness created in their home by going out and getting a job. They sublimate all the energies that should be directed to their home and their family, and they invest it into their job to make being at home more tolerable.

Join a Militant Women's Group

Some women become hostile and join a militant women's group and take their anger and frustration out on men in general because they lack the courage to confront their husband directly.

Become Depressed

Some isolate themselves, stay at home, and become depressed.

Infidelity

Some have an affair, trying to find comfort and recognition in another man.

Escape Through Drugs and Alcohol

Some drown themselves in drugs or alcohol in order to shut out the pain.

Desertion

There are a growing number of women in our generation that have decided to do what the men did in the previous generation: simply get in the car, drive away, and never come back. This is happening in the Church, too, though you wouldn't know it on Sundays. We show up, arm in arm, and are admired by everyone as lovely couples even though we've had terrible fights in the car on the way to church. I've learned that what a person is on the outside may be unrelated to what he or she is on the inside. Too many Christians are lonely and hurting emotionally, but they hide it for fear someone will know their pain.

CHARACTERISTICS OF CHRIST'S LOVE

Too many men are neglecting what God has called them to do in their role as husbands. Ephesians 5:25 deals with our responsibility to dispel the loneliness in our homes when it says, "Husbands, love your wives, just as Christ also loved the church and gave Himself for her." There are five characteristics of the love Christ has for the Church, and they should be mirrored in the love a husband has for his wife.

His Love Is Realistic

Christ's love for the Church isn't some sort of romantic sentimentalism. He loves the Church with a deep love that doesn't keep score and is not interested in mere performance. Christ loves the Church realistically, and husbands are to love their wives the same way. One thing I've learned in talking to wives who are hurting is that the relationship always seemed to move away from love and toward performance. I once received a letter from a lonely wife who said, "I never feel like I measure up. No matter what I do, it's never good enough. So our relationship seems to be a day-to-day up and down situation. When I'm good, he loves me. When I'm not, he doesn't."

Husbands, if Christ were to love you based upon your performance toward Him, where would you be? You see, God loves us in spite of our failings. That's one of the most overwhelming truths of Scripture. He didn't first love me, then find out who I really am. He loved me in spite of who I am; while I was still in my sins, He chose to die for me. That's the sort of love we are to have for our wives. Our love is to be realistic, based upon fact and not fancy. Our love includes faults and failures and all the unlovely elements that are a part of each of us. We love through those things because that's how God loves us.

One of the biggest problems young people face as they marry is their unrealistic expectations of marriage. Once they discover that married life isn't all they thought it would be, they grow disillusioned with their partner. False expectations come from watching too many movies and reading too many romance novels where love is a feeling, and everything comes together perfectly. We even describe it by saying we fell in love, as though it were a gaping hole that we unwittingly fell into as our eyes met across a crowded room. Then we wake up the next morning looking at the curlers above those eyes, and the lack of makeup around them, and reality strikes hard. One ministry the Church ought to have is to do away with the unrealistic perspectives which have developed in our culture about marriage and families. We should be holding up God's standard of marriage, which has little to do with the external beauty of an individual and much to do with the internal working of their heart. We need to be offering young people a realistic appraisal of marriage so they enter into it with their eyes open. Christ's love for the Church is realistic, and our love for our mate is to be realistic also.

His Love Is Sacrificial

"Husbands, love your wives, just as Christ also loved the church and gave Himself for her." Jesus counted the cost, then gave Himself on our behalf. His love was sacrifice, not sentiment. His love cost our Lord His life. I think too many people today want a relationship that doesn't cost anything. They have their hands out, waiting to receive, but they aren't willing to give. Marriage is a relationship of constant giving, one to the other.

I know Christian men love to hear the passage about the woman submitting, but really the Bible says we both submit to each other. There is certainly a chain of command that reflects the wife's submission to her husband, but there is also a sense in which the husband is submitting to his wife's needs in order to please and protect her. Marriage is a blending of ourselves together, the determination to sacrifice whatever we have for the sake of our loved one.

The word "sacrifice" is actually made up of two words: *sacra*, which means "holy," and *fisio*, which means "to make." When we sacrifice, we make something holy. We are to make holy the person we love. That's what Christ did for us. In love He made us holy. And husbands are to love their wives in a way that makes them holy. That sort of love will dispel loneliness. It will also cost us time and pleasure and ambition and friends, for it will impact our selfish desires and priorities. When you love someone sacrificially, you put them first. Nothing comes before them. One woman who wrote to me about her marital troubles said,

> I never wanted anything from him but himself. I wanted him to spend time with me. He gave me gifts, but they were because he felt guilty about his lack of time. He never cancelled anything for us; he always cancelled us for something else. I felt worthless, and I started resenting everything about him. That's when I realized I had become a bitter person.

Eventually that woman left her husband because she decided it was better to face all the unpleasant circumstances of a divorce than to continue along their current course. It's scary, but I've seen this pattern time after time in Christian marriages. Charles Swindoll has said that marriages don't blow out, they go flat as a result of a slow leak. And the cause of that leak is the fact that someone refused to pay the price to keep the relationship alive.

His Love Is Purposeful

Christ loved the Church in order that "He might present her to Himself a glorious church, not having spot or wrinkle or any such thing, but that she should be holy and without blemish" (Ephesians 5:27). Jesus had a purpose in His love: the development of a holy Church. And the purpose behind a man's love for his wife should be that she become all she can be as a person. The husband who tries to hold his wife back or inhibit her growth is acting in opposition to God's plan. That husband must feel threatened by her gifts and abilities and doubt his own worth, so he tries to stifle his wife. But the Bible teaches that a man who loves his wife will have the goal of helping her develop fully as a person. God's plan, husbands, is for us to invest in our wives. We are to do all we can to assist her spiritual development, her self-confidence, and the exercise of her gifts. We are trying to help her find fulfillment, putting her needs ahead of our own. Love your wife with a purpose, and help her to grow.

His Love Is Willing

Jesus Christ loves the Church willingly. He doesn't love us because we are so loveable, but because He wills to love us. That's a foreign notion to most people today. In our culture we have the idea that love takes place when we feel like it. If you don't feel like loving, you can't do it. But that's simply not true. Feeling follows action. The feeling of love will follow the action of loving. If we make the decision to love and fill our life with loving actions, the feeling will follow the will.

Let me take an example from my own life. I run most mornings. I don't run because I deeply want to. I don't get up in the morning and say, "Wow! Today I get to begin my day by running five miles!" Running is an act of the will. I get my old body moving because I know it's good for me. Once I take the action, the feeling follows. Once I get home and take a shower and relax, knowing I've done the right thing in keeping my body healthy, I get a good feeling about it. Love works the same way. The Bible says Christ loves the Church because He wants to, not because He feels like it. He wills to. If we are to love as Christ does, we must willingly choose to do so and take the action that goes along with that decision.

When Christ gave a message to the church at Ephesus in Revelation 2, He told them, "You have left your first love" (verse 4). That is, they had fallen away from God and were satisfied with simply going through the motions. There was no passion in their love. So what was the solution? "Go back and do the things you did at first." That is, go back to the beginning of the relationship and do those same things again. In a marriage, that means to take her some flowers. Pay attention to her. Take her on a date and talk to her. You'll improve the relationship, and you'll find yourself feeling better for doing it. The love that should be in both your hearts will begin to develop according to the activity of love you are involved in. Like Jesus, take the initiative to love.

His Love Is Absolute

In Ephesians 5:28 we read, "So husbands ought to love their own wives as their own bodies." The words in this verse don't merely mean that I am to love my wife as much as I love my body, but that I am to love her because she is my body. She is part of me. We are one flesh. I must love her and minister to her needs because she is a part of me. I cannot neglect an injury to my body because it hurts; for the same reason I cannot neglect my wife when she hurts. I am responsible for taking care of her, and we share a unity and oneness.

It's amazing to me how many women hurt deeply, feeling lonely because of their marriage, and their husbands don't even know it. Sometimes they will sit in my office and, in a moment of great courage, reveal their pain. Invariably the husband will say, "Honey, I didn't know you felt that way."

I pray that every day God will help me as a husband to be sensitive to the needs of my wife, to be able to see when she is hurting, and sense how she should be ministered to. I want to love her as Christ loves the Church, taking the initiative to dispel loneliness, and following the example the Lord set on Calvary.

1. In your own words, why do some people get lonely even though they are married?

    a. If you are married, have you ever endured a season of loneliness? Or simply had a lonely day? When? If it was a season, how long did it last?

    b. What counsel would you offer to a person who has complained of loneliness in their marriage?

    c. If you're not married, have you witnessed loneliness in a marriage, perhaps a marriage close to you? How did you handle it? How did it impact you?

2. Read Ephesians 5:22-33.

    a. What does this passage call for wives to do?

    b. What does this passage call for husbands to do?

    c. Define "submission" and describe how it should occur within a marriage.

    d. Describe the love a husband should have for his wife.

e. In practice, what does that love look like? How should a husband's love be displayed toward his wife? What actions and words should be evident?

3. How would you say that Christ loves His Church?

   a. What did the Lord do for the Church?

   b. What is the value of applying that to a marriage?

   c. For what reasons, do you think, does God want your marriage to reflect His love?

   d. Is there anything that can be changed or worked on in your marriage to better reflect God's love? How can you make sure you and your spouse stay committed to God and each other?

4. What further advice for marriage do you find in Colossians 3:18-21?

   a. What is the meaning of verse 19?

   b. What is the best advice you could offer a young couple preparing for marriage?

1. Take inventory of the marriages you see in your life. In your opinion, are they strong examples of Christlike love, or are they lacking something?

   a. How do the marriages in our lives impact us?

   b. When we see loneliness in another's marriage, what are we supposed to do? What should be our response?

2. When we go through a season of loneliness in our marriages, what other struggles stem from it?

   a. What good can come from seasons of loneliness in marriage?

   b. What long-lasting effects can come from seasons of loneliness?

   c. How can these struggles be overcome so God's love still prevails?

3. When a bride and groom commit to one another, they don't often think they will encounter extreme trials such as loneliness. How can we take preventive steps to make sure loneliness doesn't have a place in our marriages?

a. What do these steps look like in our daily lives?

b. If you're lonely in your marriage, does it seem like your loneliness is too great to overcome? How can you get the courage to reveal your suffering?

4. Why is the concept of Christ giving Himself for the Church so crucial in a marriage?

a. What was Christ's purpose, according to Ephesians 5:26-27?

b. If you're married, what application can you draw for your own marriage?

c. What is the meaning of verse 28?

d. How is a loving relationship described in verse 29?

e. What truth do you learn in verse 30?

5. If you have overcome a season of loneliness, what
   encouragement can you offer to the group?

DID YOU KNOW?

The passage quoted in Ephesians 5:31 is originally from
Genesis 2:24, where God first defined what marriage should
be. It's the most often quoted verse of the Bible, occurring
five times in Scripture!

THE LONELY SINGLE

1 Corinthians 7:1, 7–9, 32–35

In this lesson we'll explore the biblical directives to Christian singles.

OUTLINE

Paul wrote to the believers at Corinth and told them that being single is a good thing. Too often the Church has forgotten that lesson and made singles second-class citizens, but the Bible speaks of the many blessings of being single. Paul offers five principles for singleness that we are to put into practice in our life.

   I. Acknowledge Singleness as Good

  II. Accept Singleness as a Gift

 III. Allow Singleness for Your Growth

  IV. Activate Singleness for God

   V. Affirm Singleness With Gratitude

There are more than 121 million single adults in the United States—15 million widowed, 25 million divorced, and 81 million never married.

As we have come to recognize the explosion in the numbers of singles, one other fact has also become clear: There is still a strong desire for satisfying relationships. New enterprises have sprung up simply to meet the needs of singles, thus we've seen the advent of singles bars, computerized dating services, and even Christian ministries and worship services for singles only. Not too long ago, I saw an advertisement in a Christian newspaper that read, "God did not ordain singleness and loneliness"—then it urged people to subscribe to some kind of Christian dating service! At our church in Fort Wayne, we had a singles ministry that attracted people from a hundred miles away. It wasn't because the ministry was so great, it was simply that we had the only singles ministry in the area. We learned through that experience that singles are not primarily interested in great programs, but in being seen as individuals of worth. One woman in our body said to me, "I sit in the pew, I sing the songs, I'm in the faith; but when the service is finished, I leave as I came in—hungry for the touch of someone. I want someone to tell me that I'm a person worth something to somebody. Just a smile would do it, some sign that I am not a stranger."

One time I asked the singles in our church to write letters to me describing their lives so that I could better understand what they were experiencing. For the next few days, I was inundated with letters from singles. I came away impressed that most of them had their lives together pretty well. At the same time, I realized that many married people in the Church have misunderstood singles, and that has caused problems in our relationships with them. In Paul's first letter to the believers in Corinth, he dealt with some of the issues of being a Christian and being single. There are at least five things the apostle has to say that all Christians, married or single, should reflect on.

ACKNOWLEDGE SINGLENESS AS GOOD

Four times in 1 Corinthians 7, Paul uses the phrase "it is good" to describe singleness. In the very first verse he says, "Now concerning the things of which you wrote to me: *It is* good for a man not to touch a woman." In verse 8 he writes, "But I say to the unmarried and to the widows: It is good for them if they remain even as I am."

And later in verse 26, he says, "I suppose therefore that this is good because of the present distress—that *it is* good for a man to remain as he is." Four times he notes that singleness is good. The only thing startling about that is I find most married Christians don't believe it. I think many Christians see singles in the Church as second-class citizens, people who haven't quite arrived in maturity yet.

Often married Christians express disappointment in people, saying things like, "What's a nice guy like you doing single?" or "What's wrong with you?" or even "All you have to do is pray for a husband, and God will provide one." That sort of insensitivity drives singles away from the Church. One single woman wrote to me and asked, "Why can't people be more sensitive to where we are? Why must everything in the church revolve around husband and wife and parent and child?"

Paul makes it clear that singleness is good. If you're single, you are OK. You don't have to be different to be approved by the Lord. So acknowledge your singleness as something good. If you are married, consider your attitude toward singles, and remember that the Bible says "it is good"—it's OK!

ACCEPT SINGLENESS AS A GIFT

One of my favorite pieces of doggerel was written by some unknown single woman. It goes like this:

O unknown man, whose rib I am, why don't you come for me?
A lonely, homesick rib I am that would with others be.
I want to wed—now there, it's said. I won't deny and fib.
I want my man to come at once and claim his rib.

Some men have thought that I'd be theirs, but only for a bit.
We found out soon it wouldn't do, we didn't seem to fit.
There's just one place, the only space I'll fit.
I will not fib, I want that man to come at once and claim his rib.

Oh, don't you sometimes feel a lack, a new rib needed there?
It's I! Do come and get me soon before I have gray hair.
Come get me, dear, I'm homesick here. I want, and I'll not fib,
I want my man to come at once and claim his rib.

Many people can identify with those feelings, but if that describes your attitude, God has a gift for you. Notice what it says in 1 Corinthians 7:7: "For I wish that all men were even as I myself. But each one has his own gift from God, one in this manner and another in that." The Living Bible puts it this way: "God gives some the gift of a husband or wife, and others he gives the gift of being able to stay happily unmarried." Being married is a gift from God. Being single is also a gift from God. If you happen to be single, you need to accept your singleness as one of God's gifts to you. He knows what is best for you, and He wants you to accept your singleness as His special gift.

Over in Matthew 19:12, there is an interesting perspective shared by our Lord:

For there are eunuchs who were born thus from *their* mother's womb, and there are eunuchs who were made eunuchs by men, and there are eunuchs who have made themselves eunuchs for the kingdom of heaven's sake. He who is able to accept *it*, let him accept *it*.

In other words, some people may be single for a physical reason, some for a medical reason, and some have committed themselves to a life of celibacy for a spiritual reason. The Church of Jesus Christ would have been impoverished were it not for the great single leaders whom God has raised up over the centuries. One of the greatest missionaries in the annals of history was David Brainerd, who carried on such an intense evangelistic effort among the Native Americans early in this country's history that it took him out of this world long before his time. His ministry was such that, if he'd had a family, he could never have accomplished what God had called him to do. Many great Christians have been single by God's design, and a marriage would have precluded them from doing some of the work God had planned for them. Therefore, if you are single, view it as part of God's plan. Accept it as one of His special gifts to you.

ALLOW SINGLENESS FOR YOUR GROWTH

Paul's words in 1 Corinthians 7:26–27 are instructive: "I suppose therefore that this is good because of the present distress—that *it is* good for a man to remain as he is: Are you bound to a wife? Do not seek to be loosed. Are you loosed from a wife? Do not seek a wife." Paul isn't saying that it is wrong to look for a partner, but that getting married should not be the dominating motivation of our life. It's wrong to allow the pursuit of marriage to be the only thing we think about. Perhaps in your present situation, God is trying to teach you a concept or cause you to grow in a way you could never grow if you were married. When you allow singleness for your growth, you become content with God's plan for your life.

Christian, there is something far worse than the loneliness of being single, and that is the misery of marital discord. If you get married to the wrong person because you were unwilling to wait for God's plan to be put into operation, you will have replaced one sort of misery for another. You will long for those days of loneliness. Don't make marriage your supreme goal; make growth in Christ your supreme goal.

Not long ago you could find want ads in the "personals" section of a newspaper from people desperate to get married. We've seen the type: "Caring, sensitive man in his forties, seeks fun-loving, intelligent woman for wide range of activities." Most of those folks lived and breathed just to get married. But God says to the Christian, "I know you." He knows what you need. If you are to get married, He has a mate for you. Don't take things into your own hands. Use your singleness as a time of growth. One single woman wrote and said, "I'd rather be married than single; but for now, I know the Lord loves me and has me single. Trusting in Him and waiting on His plan is difficult; but He is my Rock, and that is more important than being married." This woman understands that God is in charge of her situation and that He is using it to help her grow. If you are single, relax in what God has for you; allow Him to help you grow.

ACTIVATE SINGLENESS FOR GOD

Paul notes in his letter to the Corinthians that a single person has certain advantages when it comes to ministry:

> I want you to be without care. He who is unmarried cares for the things of the Lord—how he may please the Lord. But he who is married cares about the things of the world—how he may please *his* wife. . . . And this I say for your own profit, not that I may put a leash on you, but for what is proper, and that you may serve the Lord without distraction (7:32–33, 35).

The single person is free from the stress and strain of a marriage and family life, and ought to see that as an advantage. My wife and I have four children, and each one adds a new dimension of stress and responsibility. You see, a married person must care for the concerns of the family. That's his or her biblical responsibility. If I don't minister to my family, I've got no right to minister to the Church. But Paul points out that a single person does not have those same stresses, and can give himself or herself fully to the work of the Lord. You can activate your singleness for things that have eternal importance to the Kingdom of God.

Every married Christian understands that. We struggle with the various priorities of life, trying to fit family and work and church and service into a balanced system. A single person doesn't have that same sort of pressure. He or she can "care for the things of the Lord" and can "serve the Lord without distraction." You can give yourself fully to God without the pressure of balancing all these other relationships. The service of God can consume your life. Those who are lonely as singles are the ones worrying about what isn't happening to them, instead of thinking about how they can minister to others. I know of a woman in our church who routinely counsels people and makes herself available day or night to talk. Many times she has been called out of bed in the middle of the night just to talk with a friend, something that would have been almost impossible if she had a husband and children. God's plan for her right now is to minister to others in a way that requires her to be single. By activating her singleness for God, and by viewing it as a positive rather than a negative, she is able to effectively minister to others.

One thing I've learned in ministry is that if you give, you get back. We have many singles in our church who arrive early, help set things up, attend worship, help with the children's classes, and stay to clean up afterward. Their availability allows them to minister in a way which many marrieds cannot, and their ministry makes them some of the happiest people in the body. By activating their singleness for the Lord, they are able to experience the joy of service.

AFFIRM SINGLENESS WITH GRATITUDE

As I've studied the problem of loneliness, I have found one truth to stand out above all others: A spirit of gratitude in our hearts will dispel a spirit of loneliness. You see, gratitude causes us to take inventory of our life; when we remember all the good things God has done on our behalf, we are reminded of the fact that loneliness is only one small part of life. God has blessed us with so many things that it is difficult to reflect on them all and still sit in self-pity.

In verses 36–40 of chapter 7, Paul gives a picture of a single lady sitting at home, under her father's authority. The family would normally arrange her marriage, but Paul simply says that if a woman is "past the flower of youth," which is to say she has gone beyond the age when a woman might normally marry in their culture, it is still fine for her to marry someone. The father can still arrange for a Christian husband, though his daughter is no longer young. Why this concern with someone mature getting married? It's Paul's way of saying, "Don't feel you've got to rush your children into marriage."

Some parents are so concerned that their kids marry, they will go to any length to arrange it. They push their sons and daughters toward the marriage altar just to get them married off, and Paul is warning that there is no harm in waiting a while. Getting married before you hit the magic age of thirty isn't a necessity for a fulfilled life.

The attitude Paul is trying to foster is one of praise for who we are and where God has put us. Paul goes on to say that if you are a widow, praise God for your situation. If you are married, praise Him. If you are single, praise Him. We don't always understand why God has chosen to do things a certain way, and we may desire a different circumstance, but we praise God anyway because He is in charge and He knows what is best. So praise Him for your circumstances. Give Him your gratitude for the opportunities that go along with your situation.

God is interested in your life. He loves you and only wants what is best for you. He wants to draw you toward Himself, and He has arranged for your situation to best foster your growth in Christ. As you examine your life, thank Him for loving you so much.

PERSONAL QUESTIONS

1. Considering where you are in your relationship journey, are you lonely? How would you describe what loneliness feels like?

    a. If anyone has tried to counsel you or comfort you in this season, what are some of the things they have said? Was it helpful?

    b. If you have married friends, is it difficult for them to connect with you because you're single?

    c. Compared to a single person, what could a married person know or understand about loneliness?

    d. What can you learn from a married person about loneliness?

    e. What do you believe God is trying to do in your life while you're single?

2. Paul wanted the Corinthians to understand that singleness was not something to be afraid of, and it's also not a reason for a person to be considered a "second-class citizen" in the Church. If you are single, what does it look like to be accepted by your brothers and sisters in Christ who are married?

   a. What is something you can say to someone, whether they are married or not, when you feel like you are not accepted in your singleness?

3. Singleness can be a gift from God for this season in your life. What is He saying to you? What desires has He laid on your heart that you know wouldn't be easy to accomplish if you were married?

   a. How can you find contentment in your relationship with Christ even if your relationship status remains single?

   b. Have you fully grasped the truth that God loves and accepts you no matter what (whether you are married or single)? If not, what is holding you back?

   c. How can you encourage other single people to keep the faith?

1. Read Philippians 4:4-13.

   a. What comfort can these Scriptures offer to us in this season of loneliness? Even if the loneliness in being single persists much longer than we anticipate, what truth can we hold onto about God's love for us?

   b. How important is it that we work to maintain a perspective in this season in life, remembering that singleness has a purpose?

   c. Although we desire to be married someday, how can we be an example of contentment in Christ?

2. For those in the group that are married, what comfort (not advice) can you offer to the singles in the group?

3. For those in the group that are well seasoned in being alone, what lessons have you learned about yourself and your relationship with Christ? What have you been able to accomplish for the kingdom of God as a single?

4. What correlation exists between accepting our single status and being content with who we are in Christ?

    a. Can we remain joyful and content if we question why God has us single right now?

5. Since being single presents unique opportunities for ministry and forming long-lasting relationships, are we taking full advantage of our singleness? Are we doing all we can to find our individual identity in Christ?

a. Why should it be important to be an individual in Christ before anything else?

b. If we are holding ourselves back from realizing and achieving the plans God has for us, what steps can we take to pursue His greater purpose as a single Christian?

6. How can we be praying for each other this week as it pertains to loneliness in a season of singleness?

DID YOU KNOW?

You can read all about one of the greatest missionaries ever (and a man who remained single) by reading *The Life of David Brainerd*. He kept a journal to help recount his days ministering to the Indian tribes of early America. This man, who spoke only English, set out at the age of nineteen with the conviction that the Native Americans were lost men and women in need of the Savior. He led more than 10,000 to a saving knowledge of Jesus Christ before dying of tuberculosis, brought on by the severe weather he endured, at the age of 29.

THE LONELY SAINTS

Jeremiah 15:17–18

In this lesson we'll learn about the loneliness Christians experience.

OUTLINE

Everyone experiences loneliness at times. Even some of the most famous people in Scripture faced lonely times and difficult situations. A quick review of the Bible reveals a number of people who have experienced loneliness.

I. Loneliness and the Bible

II. God Ministers to the Lonely

The prophet Jeremiah wrote,

I did not sit in the assembly of the mockers, nor did I rejoice; I sat alone because of Your hand, for You have filled me with indignation. Why is my pain perpetual and my wound incurable, which refuses to be healed? Will You surely be to me like an unreliable stream, as waters *that* fail? (15:17–18)

Here was a man who loved God and served Him faithfully, but felt the full effect of being left alone because of his service. Did you know that most widows say that loneliness is the worst problem they face in life? Or that 25 percent of unmarried men claim that intense loneliness is their biggest concern? When asked about the connection between loneliness and health, a doctor replied, "That's like asking about the connection between air and health." [1]

Like the air we breathe, human companionship is a necessity. It is sometimes taken for granted, but when we face social isolation or the sudden loss of love, our loneliness can significantly contribute to illness. What is loneliness? I don't know how to define it; all I can do is describe it. It's an underlying anxiety, a sharp ache in a moment of grief, and an empty feeling in the pit of the stomach. For some it is a long period of stress that wears them down. There is no anguish like loneliness. I have read it in the letters from prisoners who listen to our radio broadcast, heard it in the voices on the phone, and seen it in the faces of those who have just buried a loved one. I ache with its effects as I hug grandparents at the funeral of a beautiful young child, snatched from their presence after a few short hours of violent, unexplainable disease. I observe the seeming cruelty of loneliness in the faces of many single people trying to find community and fellowship in a family-oriented world. I have even seen it in the eyes of my wife, when the ministry to which God has called me separates us for many nights in a row.

We have all listened to the music of loneliness, from Hank Williams singing "I'm So Lonesome I Could Cry" to the Beatles chorus of "all the lonely people, where do they all come from?" Samuel Taylor Coleridge's "Rime of the Ancient Mariner" summarizes loneliness better than anything I could say, when it goes: "Alone, alone, all, all alone. Alone on a wide, wide sea. And never a saint took pity on my soul in agony." [2] Thousands of lives are summarized by that poem. Even the psalmist David must have felt that way when he wrote, "No man cared for my soul."

LONELINESS AND THE BIBLE

What has happened to us? Why can't we be close to others emotionally when we are so close physically? I was surprised at what I found when I opened my Bible and began looking for loneliness. Though the word "lonely" appears nowhere in Scripture, the pages are filled with illustrations about people who battled loneliness for a number of reasons. For example, in the book of Genesis we find Enoch, a man who was set apart from his contemporaries. In a wicked and sinful world, Enoch walked with God. He must have been a terribly lonely man. On his heels came Noah, to whom was given the absurd task of building a large, seagoing vessel well away from any source of water. He carried out his task over a number of years, the subject of abuse by all. But Hebrews tells us that Noah walked by faith.

A favorite vignette of loneliness can be found in Genesis 16. Since Abram's wife Sarai could bear no children, she gave her servant Hagar to Abram for a wife. But when Hagar became pregnant, a bitter hatred came between those two women. Hagar was banished and fled to the wilderness. When we read the biblical account of Hagar weeping by a fountain, far away from family and friends, we get a picture of extreme loneliness.

When Abraham trudged up Mount Moriah with his son Isaac to carry out the unexplained instruction of God, we get a feel for the loneliness and isolation that must have overtaken him. When Moses was banished from Pharaoh's kingdom to the wilderness of Midian, trading the royal court for a shepherd's life at the back of the desert, he must have experienced a deep, painful loneliness. And when David was overwhelmed with the problems of the kingdom, he would pour out his loneliness to God in poetry, writing,

> My heart is stricken and withered like grass, so that I forget
> to eat my bread. Because of the sound of my groaning my
> bones cling to my skin. I am like a pelican of the wilderness;
> I am like an owl of the desert. I lie awake, and am like a
> sparrow alone on the housetop (Psalm 102:4–7).

Job is one of the loneliest men in Scripture. He reflects on his sufferings, but never finds a receptive response. All his counselors turn away from him, and even his wife tells him "to curse God and die." In the midst of his loneliness, he feels as though even God has deserted him. Perhaps that is how some of the New Testament believers felt after their Savior had been taken from them and the whole world turned against them. The apostle Paul told Timothy that "all men forsook me." Many of the disciples were martyred for the sake of the Gospel, dying alone for the cause of Christ.

Even the Lord Jesus Christ suffered the loneliness that so many people today feel. He warned His disciples that "the hour is coming, yes, has now come, that you will be scattered, each to his own, and will leave Me alone" (John 16:32). He not only experienced human loneliness, but as the Son of God, He lived with the knowledge that the cross was coming. He knew beforehand that one day He would experience the feeling of being abandoned by the Father on the cross. In the closing days of His life, as He prayed in the Garden of Gethsemane, Jesus agonized in prayer over what was coming. But He prayed alone, for none of His followers could even stay awake for an hour to pray with Him. Later, as He hung on that cross on Golgotha, our Savior experienced the maximum impact of loneliness. His friends had abandoned and betrayed Him, and the Father had turned His back. In the agony and aloneness of the moment, Jesus cried out, "My God, My God, why have You forsaken Me?" In those moments, Christ experienced the loneliness of a Christless eternity for each one of us. That loneliness is beyond description. Our Lord and Savior can understand your loneliness, for He has experienced it Himself!

All the loneliness experienced in Scripture makes it hard to swallow the testimony of those who say, "I'm never lonely because I have Jesus with me." Every time I hear words like that, I get the impression they're saying what they think they ought to say, rather than what they feel. The Bible doesn't say we are never to feel lonely. In fact, it offers testimony of great men and women of faith who experienced real loneliness. We dare not deny it. Friends and family pass away, and we feel lonely. We get old or sick and we feel all alone, facing the terror of being alone at death. But if we know Christ, we are part of the family of God; as we reach out to those around us, we discover that the loneliness goes away. The Bible is filled with the testimonies of lonely people who were met by God in the midst of their loneliness.

GOD MINISTERS TO THE LONELY

As I read through my Bible, studying passage after passage about lonely people facing difficult circumstances, I began to discover something. Every time we find the testimony of a lonely person in Scripture, we also see, in the midst of their loneliness, the Lord break through in some unique and special way. It's almost as if the Lord were saying, "Don't fight it. I'll be there for you." For instance, when Hagar sat weeping next to the fountain, God reached out to her. "Then she called the name of the LORD who spoke to her, You-Are-The-God-Who-Sees; for she said, 'Have I also here seen Him who sees me?' Therefore the well was called Beer Lahai Roi," which means "the Well of the One Who Lives and Sees Me" (Genesis 16:13–14). Hagar, in the wilderness all by herself, met God. Though banished by her friends and separated from her family, God broke into her life. She was so excited, she named the place after a God who loved her so much that He came to her in her loneliness.

The story of Abraham is similar. God broke in upon Abraham's experience to reveal Himself to His obedient servant. Just as Abraham was about to sacrifice his long-awaited son,

> The Angel of the LORD called to him from heaven and said, "Abraham, Abraham!" So he said, "Here I am." And He said, "Do not lay your hand on the lad, or do anything to him; for now I know that you fear God, since you have not withheld your son, your only *son*, from Me." Then Abraham lifted his eyes and looked, and there behind *him* was a ram caught in a thicket by its horns. So Abraham went and took the ram, and offered it up for a burnt offering instead of his son. And Abraham called the name of the place, The-LORD-Will-Provide; as it is said *to* this day, "In the Mount of the LORD it shall be provided" (Genesis 22:11–14).

On the mountain of Abraham's loneliness, God provided. In Abraham's deepest need, God broke through into his experience. At least two places in the Old Testament world are named as monuments to a God who cares about lonely people. These places today have a name to remind us that when we are alone and away from God and when we feel forsaken by everyone, God is still there. If we will just wait, He will make His presence known at the moment we need Him most.

This same pattern holds true in the life of Moses. He wandered in the desert of Midian, away from all that he knew. But it is in this experience, while alone in the desert, that God speaks to Moses and reveals Himself through the burning bush. In his loneliness, Moses hears the Lord say, "I am here, and I want you to serve Me." Have you ever considered what would have happened if Moses had not been alone where God could get his attention and minister to his need? God uses our loneliness to draw us toward Himself, to minister to us, and to reveal Himself to us in our moment of need.

The story of Job is no different. He met God in the midst of his loneliness. In the middle of a tragic, broken life, the Lord was suddenly no longer absent. "I have heard of You by the hearing of the ear," Job says to the Lord in Job 42:5, "but now my eye sees You." Before these awful experiences, Job had heard all about God. But now, in the midst of his trouble, he sees that God is with him. King David learned the same lesson, for he not only wrote poems about being lonely, he is the man who wrote, "The LORD *is* my Shepherd; I shall not want. . . . Yea, though I walk through the valley of the shadow of death, I will fear no evil; for You *are* with me" (Psalm 23:1, 4). In the middle of his loneliness, David discovered anew that God was on his side. "The LORD *is* my light and my salvation; whom shall I fear?" (Psalm 27:1) God ministered to David in his time of need; He broke into David's life when he was lonely.

To the lonely disciples in the New Testament who feared being left alone without their Savior, Jesus said,

> Let not your heart be troubled; you believe in God, believe also in Me. In My Father's house are many mansions; if *it* were not *so*, I would have told you. I go to prepare a place for you. And if I go and prepare a place for you, I will come again and receive you to Myself; that where I am, *there* you may be also (John 14:1–3).

The Lord took care of their future, reminding them that one day they would be together again. He also took care of their present by promising to send a Comforter to be with them after He had physically gone. In their loneliness, the Holy Spirit came eternally into their hearts, never to be separated from them.

How like the precious Lord this is, to tell us about others who have hurt, and to reveal to us how He helped them. When Paul complained to Timothy that no one had been with him at his trial, he also noted that "the Lord stood with me and strengthened me" (2 Timothy 4:17). As clearly as God saw Hagar, He sees you. The God who provided for Abraham will provide for you. The God who revealed Himself to Moses will also reveal Himself to you. The God who spoke to Job speaks to you today. He is your Shepherd as well as King David's; the Comforter promised by Jesus Christ comforts you. If He lives within your heart, He stands with you, just as He stood with Paul at his trial. This Christ, who experienced the ultimate loneliness, will provide mercy and grace to you in your time of need. He waits for you in your prayers.

Notes

1. James J. Lynch, interview with Christopher Anderson, *People Magazine*, 22 August 1977:30.

2. *Harvard Classics*, Vol. 41 (New York: P. E. Collier and Son, 1910), 698–717.

1. What causes loneliness for you and the ones you know and love?

   a. What are some of your fears when facing loneliness? Are you ever afraid you won't make it through, or that God will abandon you? What are your thoughts?

   b. Why does loneliness persist in the world?

   c. Is there a biblical reason to believe God would allow a season of loneliness to persist without a purpose? Why or why not?

   d. For those who do not follow Christ, is there relief from their loneliness? How does that differ from the relief you have?

2. How does loneliness manifest itself in your life? What does it look like?

   a. Does your loneliness pull you closer to Christ? How?

3. Loneliness tends to be the silent moments where God reveals His presence to you. How is God revealing His plan for you right now, even if only one detail at a time?

   a. How has His constant presence been a comfort for you?

   b. There are monuments in the Old Testament that were named in remembrance that God is always with those who feel lonely. What are the monuments in your life?

4. Moses, Abraham, Hagar, and Job are only a few Old Testament examples of how God reveals Himself in loneliness. How can their stories encourage you?

   a. How can you use their stories to encourage your lonely loved ones?

   b. What would you or a loved one need to hear in times of loneliness?

5. Does the pain of loneliness ever become physical for you?

   a. In the moments when the pain seems unbearable, how can you seek solace in God's presence?

   b. When you doubt God's presence is surrounding you, how do you still cling to Him?

1. Despite being digitally connected in society, why is it easy for us to be emotionally lonely? Why is it difficult to find people we can truly connect with?

   a. What influences exist in our world that can worsen, if not cause, our loneliness to persist?

   b. What is God trying to do in our lives that will bring us closer to Him?

2. Who should be our biblical influences in overcoming our seasons of loneliness?

   a. What did God do in those stories that we should commit to memory?

b. Looking back, what has God done, and is He doing, in our seasons of loneliness to make Himself more real to us?

3. In our loneliness, we should remember that there is a purpose for our pain and that God has a lesson for us to learn. What barriers might exist that prevent us from learning something valuable?

4. Since God communicates with each of us on an individual level, how can our lessons encourage one another?

5. In this lesson we learned about many people in the Old Testament who suffered from feeling alone. But we also learned that Jesus Himself suffered the same lonely pain. Why would God allow Jesus to experience this pain?

a. What does it teach us about God's provision during loneliness?

b. Does God the Father ever walk away from us? Does He ever leave us? Why not?

c. How is it an act of mercy and love toward us that God shared His Son's story with us?

6. How can we remind each other through our season of solitude that we are never actually alone?

DID YOU KNOW?

Hagar and Abraham followed a rich tradition in naming sites after the Lord. There are more than two dozen sites named in Scripture by followers of God, commemorating His faithfulness. Some of those sites can still be seen today!

THE LONELY SENIOR

Joshua 14

In this lesson we'll explore the unique needs of older Christians.

OUTLINE

One of the elder statesmen of Scripture, Caleb, continued his leadership and ministry late in life, accomplishing some of his greatest achievements after his 85th birthday! The three keys to Caleb's success were simple.

I. **Lessons From Caleb**
   A. You Can Accomplish Life's Greatest Accomplishment at Old Age
   B. You Never Retire From the Lord's Service

II. **Secrets From Caleb's Life**
   A. He Kept Growing Physically
   B. He Kept Growing Mentally
   C. He Kept Growing Spiritually

A number of years ago my father, who was an avid photographer, decided to pull all the old photos out after our Christmas dinner and show them to everyone. It was a great joy to see the pictures of our children when they were little and to see the photographic evidence of their growth, but it was depressing to look at the pictures of myself and watch my hair turn white and my body change. I was confronted with proof that I'm getting older, and I didn't like it. We don't seem to talk much about aging in our culture, probably for fear we'll have to admit we are all getting older. Actually, there are more seniors over the age of 65 in the United States than ever before, some 54 million.[1] And medical science tells us that if we could solve the problem of arteriosclerosis, the senior population would rise dramatically. Geriatrics is one of the fastest-growing specialties in the medical world, and we're seeing more and more political activism from senior citizens and retired groups. Those of us who are Christians ought to know about aging and be ready to minister to the unique needs of the older saints. But I fear that older Christians are becoming lost in the shuffle. They are not immune to the sting of loneliness, and many suffer from the gnawing feeling of unimportance in a society that no longer needs them. The difference that growing older in Christ ought to make is often not visible.

Not too long ago I sat down to reflect on the older Christian men in my life. Many of the Christian leaders I had grown up with, who had been guests in my home, are now bitter old men who feel life has passed them by. There are a few gracious, positive models, but not many. Instead of maximizing their powers at a time when they have all sorts of experience to share, many Christians have considered themselves retired and thus make almost no impact for God. After I thought about that for a while, I said to myself, "Jeremiah, I don't want that to happen to you. I don't want to grow old like that." So I spent time in my Bible looking for positive examples of older believers. That's when I came across the man named Caleb.

LESSONS FROM CALEB

Caleb is one of the two spies sent into the Promised Land who recommended that Israel invade and take the land. He and Joshua were the only two adults allowed to survive the years of wandering in the wilderness and actually enter the Promised Land. Caleb was a man of vision and faith, and even in his autumn years he was active for the Lord. In Joshua 14 we read about Caleb being 85 years of age but still growing spiritually. When it was time for the nation of Israel to divide the land, old Caleb didn't sit around and wait for somebody else to do the work. He was right in the thick of things. He took on the leadership role that his people needed from him. As he prepared for the greatest moment of his life, he illustrates some very important lessons that I hope we will never forget.

You Can Accomplish Life's Greatest Accomplishment at Old Age

First, I believe that we can have our greatest moments in life at an age most people consider "over the hill." Lesson number one from the life of Caleb is that we can achieve life's greatest accomplishments at an old age. Even though he was 85 years old, he was involved in the greatest adventure he'd ever known. Israel was taking the land God had promised so many years earlier, and Caleb wanted to be a part of it.

You Never Retire From the Lord's Service

Lesson number two is similar: We never retire from the Lord's service. Caleb's age didn't get in the way of his job. Rather than retire and sit around, Caleb figured he would work until he was called home by the Lord.

SECRETS FROM CALEB'S LIFE

As we think about growing older, I'd like to suggest three secrets from the life of Caleb, three principles that explain his vitality in old age.

He Kept Growing Physically

Caleb was a man who took care of his body. In Joshua 14:10–11, we read Caleb saying these words:

And now, behold, the LORD has kept me alive, as He said, these forty-five years, ever since the LORD spoke this word to Moses while Israel wandered in the wilderness; and now, here I am this day, eighty-five years old. As yet I *am as* strong this day as on the day that Moses sent me; just as my strength *was* then, so now *is* my strength for war, both for going out and for coming in.

Caleb was as strong at 85 as he had been at forty! He kept his physical prowess. It reminds me of the statement we have concerning Moses in Deuteronomy 34:7, that "his eyes were not dim nor his natural vigor diminished." Remember, that was written about the prophet Moses when he was 120 years old.

Christians have a tendency to downplay the importance of the outward man. We are sometimes so spiritually-minded we forget that whatever we do spiritually we have to do from within our physical bodies. I once saw a sign that read, "When you wear out this body, then where are you going to live?" Everything we do spiritually is done in the body. If we're going to be useful to God for many years, we've got to come to grips with what it means to grow old, and we've got to keep growing physically. Our world likes to cover growing old with humor—putting up signs that say things like "You know you're growing old, when that gleam in your eye is the sun hitting your bifocals" and "You know you're growing old when the only names in your little black book end in 'M.D.'" We don't know what to do with aging, so we poke fun at it. The songwriter Woody Guthrie described it this way:

Since I have retired from life's competition,
Each day is filled with complete repetition.
I get up each morning and dust off my wits,
Open the paper, read the obits.
If I'm not there, I know I'm not dead,
So I eat a good breakfast and go back to bed.
How do I know my youth is all spent,
My get up and go has got up and went.

There is nothing wrong with taking a lighthearted approach to aging, but I wonder if we've pushed it so far away that we cannot talk seriously about it. The Bible says that Caleb kept growing physically so that he was able to do at 85 what he did at forty. That intrigues me, since at 85 I'd like to be doing for the Lord what I was doing at forty. Apparently Caleb made some decisions when he was forty that affected his effectiveness at 85. That's truly amazing because he had every reason in the world to give up at age forty, the age when most men begin to give up on their bodies. At that time Caleb was passed over for promotion. When Moses died, the top leadership job went to Joshua, not Caleb. Had he been like many men, realizing there would be no more opportunities for him, it would have been easy to become discouraged. But he didn't; Caleb pressed on with the Lord. That was also the time Caleb was transferred to a really crummy location. At forty, he was at the peak of his career, ready to take the land promised to Israel. Instead, God put him on the back side of a desert for the next 45 years, waiting for the rebellious Jewish generation to die off so that God could finally take Israel into the Promised Land. There would seem to be no realistic, positive goal to motivate Caleb—he knew he was stuck walking around in the wilderness for a long time, waiting. His life was trapped, waiting for God's judgment to be meted out on those rebellious people.

After years of fighting in Canaan, God kept Caleb alive. Bitterness and unbelief never seemed to enter his life. His powers were at their peak. He stayed fresh with God through that difficult middle time. It's easy to run the first mile of a marathon, and in the last mile you know you're almost done, but those middle miles can be an awfully tough test. Caleb passed the test. He had made some long-lasting decisions when he was forty, and that allowed God to use him when he was 85. Instead of quitting, he kept himself ready.

John Wesley was a man like Caleb. At 85 years of age, he said he was not weary of travel. In those days before modern transportation, John Wesley traveled 250,000 miles on horseback, preached 40,000 sermons, wrote 400 books, and spoke eleven languages. He attributed his youthful vigor to exercise, getting plenty of sleep, rising at 4 A.M., and preaching at 5 A.M. every day of the week. At age 86, Wesley was annoyed that he couldn't write more than fifteen hours a day, and at 87 he confessed to an urge to lie in bed after 5:30 in the morning. Like Caleb, John Wesley took care of his body; he kept himself growing physically.

He Kept Growing Mentally

At age 85, Caleb told everyone,

Now therefore, give me this mountain of which the LORD spoke in that day; for you heard in that day how the Anakim *were* there, and *that* the cities were great *and* fortified. It may be that the LORD *will be* with me, and I shall be able to drive them out as the LORD said (Joshua 14:12).

Late in life, Caleb wanted the biggest challenge of all. Keep in mind that all the other men assigned to take the Promised Land were younger than Caleb, for the old had all died in the wilderness. Yet he wanted the mountain where the giants lived, the fellows who had so frightened the spies and the people years earlier. He was the oldest man, but he asked for the toughest job. Why? Because he still had the desire to meet a challenge. Caleb kept growing mentally. He had a dream, and he wanted to be working on it right to the end. Joshua, his contemporary, was "old, advanced in years" (Joshua 13:1), but there still remained land to be possessed. All those younger guys hadn't completed the job. They were charged with going in, clearing out the inhabitants, and settling the land; but chapters 13–16 reveal that they had failed in their duty. As a matter of fact, in Joshua 17:16, these guys complained, "The mountain country is not enough for us; and all the Canaanites who dwell in the land of the valley have chariots of iron, *both those* who *are* of Beth Shean and its towns and *those* who *are* of the Valley of Jezreel." Nobody else could get it done, so Caleb took on the job. The results are clear: "Caleb drove out the three sons of Anak from there" (15:14). He then promised his daughter in marriage to the man who could defeat the city of Kirjath Sepher, and his motivated men conquered everything in their domain. At 85 years of age, he accomplished all the goals set out for him.

Caleb had been a positive, goal-oriented person from the days he had encouraged the nation of Israel to take the Promised Land. While everyone else was thinking of an excuse, Caleb was saying, "With God we can do it!" As he aged, he didn't change. He was a brave man among cowards, a tough man among weaklings, and a positive man among negative influencers. He never stopped accepting challenges, for he knew that God's support is not bound to the years of time. When you stop dreaming, life is over.

The greatest aerial troop of our generation was the Flying Wallendas. Their patriarch, Carl Wallenda, recruited and trained his own family members to perform daring high wire acts at circuses, always without a safety net. They became famous for creating a living pyramid high on a wire with no net under them. One terrible day, when Carl Wallenda was in his seventies, the pyramid fell, killing two and injuring two others for life. Just a few days later, the family was back performing again. When asked why he would go back to such a dangerous position after experiencing such a tragedy, Wallenda replied, "To be on the wire is life. All else is waiting." He never lost the joy of the risk. Like Caleb, he kept growing mentally by taking on new challenges, setting new goals, and not allowing his age or circumstances to stop him.

He Kept Growing Spiritually

When Caleb was forty, God said this about him: "But My servant Caleb, because he has a different spirit in him and has followed Me fully, I will bring into the land where he went, and his descendants shall inherit it" (Numbers 14:24). As a young man, he was following the Lord fully, and that spirit did not diminish as he aged. At 85 he could say,

Nevertheless my brethren who went up with me made the heart of the people melt, but I wholly followed the LORD my God. So Moses swore on that day, saying, "Surely the land where your foot has trodden shall be your inheritance and your children's forever, because you have wholly followed the LORD my God" (Joshua 14:8–9).

Caleb was a man deeply committed to God. He didn't just follow the Lord until retirement age, but continued to serve God until the day he died. I've seen too many older Christians decide to take it easy; they've done their work so they step aside and wait for the younger generation to pick up the slack. That's not a biblical concept, and it certainly flies in the face of Caleb's example.

When we stop serving God, we stop growing spiritually. We stop being involved in what God has for us. We lose the edge on our spiritual life. I don't know any Christians who can sit back, retired from all Christian service, and maintain a vital and healthy relationship with God. Involvement is part of our spiritual growth, and it doesn't stop no matter how old you are.

There was something unique about the life of Caleb. He was 85 years old, but still growing. He remembered God's promises to him, and lived his life in response to them. Getting old has little to do with how we are perceived outwardly, but everything to do with what's happening to our inward life. Caleb served the Lord, and it kept him fresh physically, mentally, and spiritually.

Note

1. U.S. Census Bureau, 2019 American Community Survey. Statistics rounded to the nearest million. These statistics have been updated since this message was preached.

1. Do you have anyone in your life who falls into the category of a lonely senior?

    a. What does their life look like on the outside as they spend time with you and others?

    b. Do they still work to lead a vibrant life, or do they appear to struggle with their significance in this world?

    c. How are they an example to you as you both grow older?

    d. Do they inspire you to keep growing spiritually regardless of your age? Why or why not?

    e. What value is there in having older Christians around you?

2. What fears, if any, do you have about growing older? Are they anything like what was discussed in this lesson?

   a. What reassurance about age does Caleb's life offer?

   b. Society, relatives, and friends can sometimes make you believe you should accomplish everything while you are young. How does Caleb's story, or maybe even your own story, contradict this belief?

   c. How do you know God can use you regardless of your age or the condition of your body?

   d. How does this knowledge give you peace with where you are in your life and walk with Christ right now?

3. If you have lonely seniors in your life, how can you help to alleviate some of their pain?

4. If you are a senior and experiencing loneliness, how can Caleb's story be an example to you?

    a. Knowing you don't have to stop growing once you hit a certain age, how can you make sure you stay sharp?

    b. How can you keep yourself from growing spiritually tired as you grow older?

    c. Why should your spiritual vitality be as important, and more so, than your physical vitality?

    d. How can you be an example to younger believers in this season of life?

GROUP QUESTIONS

1. How does society's view of seniors influence our view of ourselves?

   a. As most of us have goals that we want to accomplish, is it better to achieve them quickly while we're young, or is there something to learn about taking our time?

   b. Is age simply a number?

   c. What reasons still exist, even in our older years, for us to set and accomplish goals?

d. Recalling Caleb's mentality and desire to accept challenges in his old age, what can we accomplish for Christ as we grow older?

2. Although some of us may still be considered young, most of us have people in our lives who are even younger than we are. How can we be examples to them regardless of our age?

a. What standards do we hold ourselves to when it comes to being role models and strong Christian examples to the young people in our lives?

b. What examples do we have to follow, not only in our personal lives but also in the Bible?

3. When we are older, what do we want our loved ones to say about us?

   a. How can we set ourselves up now to become that person our loved ones can admire and look up to even after we are gone?

4. As all of us will surely have a physical ailment or two to fight against as we grow older, how can we make sure our spirits stay strong?

   a. How can we keep ourselves dedicated to Christ and ready to take on any task He puts before us?

b. How have we been an example of this faithfulness to Christ so far?

c. How can we improve?

DID YOU KNOW?

The name "Caleb" is ancient, and probably means "dog." The image of someone with this name was that he would be fierce in battle, biting and snarling like an attack dog, and that he would be extremely loyal. Caleb, Joshua's second-in-command who drove the giants from the Promised Land, was aptly named.

God's Human Cure for Loneliness

1 Samuel 18:1–4

In this lesson we'll explore the friendship of two men, and how it became the cure for loneliness.

OUTLINE

David and Jonathan were friends who grew closer over time. Their friendship filled a need in their lives, driving out loneliness. Some of the characteristics of their friendship are ones we can emulate today.

I. **David and Jonathan's Committed Friendship**
   A. Friendship Is Selective
   B. Friendship Is Sacrificial
   C. Friendship Is Steadfast
   D. Friendship Is Secure

II. **Christ's Committed Friendship With Us**
   A. He Selected Us
   B. He Sacrificed for Us
   C. His Steadfast Friendship With His Father
   D. He Gives Security

I looked for some good definitions of friendship recently, and they're hard to come by. It seems that everybody has a different definition of what a friend is. But I liked one that was written by a thirteen-year-old girl: "A friend is one in front of whom you can be your own true self." That's true—a friend banishes the loneliness by allowing us to share ourselves with someone else. Ralph Waldo Emerson once wrote that a friend "is one who will make us do what we can when we are saying we can't . . . I do with my friends as I do with my books; I would have them where I could find them, but I seldom use them." The ancient philosopher Cicero noted that "friendship is the only thing in the world concerning the usefulness of which all mankind is agreed."

The Bible has much to say about friendship. For example, in Proverbs 17:17, King Solomon noted that "A friend loves at all times," and in 18:24 he wrote, "A man *who has* friends must himself be friendly, but there is a friend *who* sticks closer than a brother." Solomon's father, King David, had such a friend. He was extremely close to Jonathan, the son of King Saul; they pledged their lives to one another. In 1 Samuel 18:1–4, we read,

> Now when he had finished speaking to Saul, the soul of Jonathan was knit to the soul of David, and Jonathan loved him as his own soul. Saul took him that day, and would not let him go home to his father's house anymore. Then Jonathan and David made a covenant, because he loved him as his own soul. And Jonathan took off the robe that *was* on him and gave it to David, with his armor, even to his sword and his bow and his belt.

If you survey your life, you'll probably discover that you have four different kinds of friends. First, you have contact friends, those acquaintances whom you see every day in passing. Next you have casual friends, those with whom you share common interests. The third level of friends are your close friends, those with whom you share a common goal. But the closest kind of friend is rare: a committed friend, who loves you enough to help you grow.

DAVID AND JONATHAN'S COMMITTED FRIENDSHIP

A committed friend is willing to confront you in love over a blind spot in your life. Hopefully, if you are married, your spouse is a committed friend. Whatever level of friend you are pursuing now, there is probably no better example of a committed friendship than the one between David and Jonathan. It serves as an example to all of us who would be a committed friend, and it's a shame our culture has made such improper suggestions about two men becoming close friends. I refuse to let this culture dictate to me how I'm going to live, for I have close male friends and I thank God for them. David and Jonathan illustrate for us in a beautiful way the kind of close, rich relationship that can be had between two friends. There are some characteristics of their friendship that we should keep in mind.

Friendship Is Selective

As you read about David and Jonathan, you realize they chose to be friends. Do you know how the relationship got started? David, the son of Jesse the shepherd, took some food to his brothers who were fighting in the Israeli army against the army of the Philistines. Those Philistines had plagued Israel for months, and no one quite seemed to know what to do about them because they had a champion of war by the name of Goliath. He would stand in front of Israel's lines and shout threats, but no one was willing to go fight him. When young David saw this giant scorning God's people, he volunteered to be Israel's champion. After they got over their shock, they laughed and tried to send him home, but David just went out with his slingshot and five smooth stones. You know the rest: He cut off Goliath's head and paraded it in front of the people of God. Jonathan, the son of the king, watched David come home from the battle parading Goliath's head, and was impressed. He respected David as one soldier respects another, and the Bible says that "his soul was knit to the soul of David." That is, they were much alike, and somehow they connected emotionally to the point that they became closer than brothers. It was a relationship that would go through tremendous pressure, as Jonathan's father became jealous of David and tried to kill him on several occasions.

It's interesting that Jonathan would select David as his friend. I'm glad God allows us to pick our own friends, for often we'll become close to somebody very different from ourselves. Others will look and wonder, "How did those two ever become close?" But the answer is that somewhere, someone made a choice, a selection of friends. Lord Brook was so happy to be a friend of Sir Philip Sydney that he had his tombstone engraved with the words, "Here lies the friend of Sir Philip Sydney." Friendship is selective—we choose who will be our friends.

Friendship Is Sacrificial

In the text we see that Jonathan gave David gifts of clothes. That is significant because Jonathan, the son of the king, took off the garments which spoke of his royal heritage and gave them to his rival. Though Jonathan by right was heir to the throne, he recognized that David was God's selection to lead Israel. David's valor, leadership, and intimacy with God brought him to the place of authority; Jonathan, in a moment of symbolism, took off his royal robes and placed them on David. It was a moment of true sacrifice, and it shows the friendship and love the two men had for each other.

David was the son of a shepherd, Jonathan the firstborn of a king. David was clothed in shepherd's rags, Jonathan in royal garments. But friendship does not depend on status. Some of the most beautiful and romantic novels have been written of the relationships princes and princesses have had with the peons and paupers of the land. When Jonathan stripped himself of his royalty in favor of his rival, he took off the robe that would have one day been his as king of Israel, and gave it to the one God had chosen. In 1 Samuel 23:16–17, something important happened between the two men:

> Then Jonathan, Saul's son, arose and went to David in the woods and strengthened his hand in God. And he said to him, "Do not fear, for the hand of Saul my father shall not find you. You shall be king over Israel, and I shall be next to you. Even my father Saul knows that."

You see, Jonathan had already made up his mind that the transfer of power would take place. He had already acknowledged the kingship of David, and he accepted the fact he would not be king, but would be the one next to the king.

If you have a committed friend, you know the one ingredient which makes that friendship different from all others is the willingness to sacrifice. When we really love someone, we are willing to sacrifice for their best interest. Friendship without sacrifice is no friendship at all.

Friendship Is Steadfast

The most interesting thing in David and Jonathan's friendship is that it was not marred by the poor relationship between David and Saul. Somehow through all the strain and stress of Saul's attempts to wipe David out, Jonathan was able to stand between the two rivals and lose touch with neither of them. He was as faithful to his father as he could be, and he was a loyal and steadfast friend to David. There was no attempt on his part to manipulate his father in order to protect David, and no attempt to manipulate his friend to gain advantage for his father.

One of the privileges I've had over the years is to worship with many professional athletes from the various San Diego sports teams, and I've come to know many of these men on a personal level. Almost without exception they have told me how difficult it is for them to develop close friends. They have a tough time determining who is truly a friend and who simply wants something from them. And I think it's easy for anyone, if they're not careful, to manipulate friendships for their own purposes. C. S. Lewis, the famous Christian author and scholar, developed a number of lifelong friendships while a student at Oxford. Several in that close circle became authors, and over the years they would get together to talk and read to each other. They would talk about their works in progress, and sharpen each other "as iron sharpens iron." Two of the men in that group were Neville Caugill and Owen Barfield, both writers, though neither as prolific nor as famous as Lewis. Yet both would say that they never sensed any difference in their relationship with Lewis as he became more popular and more famous. Barfield once wrote, "I never recall a single remark, not a single word or silence, not a single look which would go to suggest that he felt his opinion was entitled to more respect than that of his old friends." I wonder how many famous men this could truthfully be said about. There was no manipulation—the same kind of friendship Jonathan shared with David.

It is too easy to build one friendship on the ruins of another. It is a common practice for teenagers to flee from one friend in order to gain the friendship of another. But true friendship doesn't work that way, and David and Jonathan illustrate that point.

Friendship Is Secure

1. It Warns

What is a friend to do if he sees you making a mistake? It is often not possible for a casual friend to say anything; he doesn't have your trust. So if a man is without friends, who will warn him of the trouble ahead? A few years back, our ministry went through some very tough times in terms of relationships, and inevitably I had people coming to me and saying, "I knew something was wrong, but I never went to talk to him. I just didn't have the courage to do it." If we are truly committed friends, we will always warn the friend in danger.

In 1 Samuel 19, when David was being hunted by King Saul, we read:

> Now Saul spoke to Jonathan his son and to all his servants, that they should kill David; but Jonathan, Saul's son, delighted greatly in David. So Jonathan told David, saying, "My father Saul seeks to kill you. Therefore please be on your guard until morning, and stay in a secret *place* and hide" (verses 1-2).

Jonathan's best friend was in danger, so he was willing to take a stand between the danger and his friend. Those are the friends I want to have, the kind that are willing to straighten me out and warn me of the danger. True friendship gives security to one's life.

2. It Intercedes

Jonathan not only warned his friend, he interceded on his friend's behalf. He was willing to plead with his father for the life of his friend. The passage in 1 Samuel continues:

> "And I will go out and stand beside my father in the field where you *are*, and I will speak with my father about you. Then what I observe, I will tell you." Thus Jonathan spoke well of David to Saul his father, and said to him, "Let not the king sin against his servant, against David, because he has not sinned against you, and because his works *have been* very good toward you. For he took his life in his hands and killed the Philistine, and the LORD brought about a great deliverance for all Israel. You saw *it* and rejoiced. Why then will you sin against innocent blood, to kill David without a cause?" So Saul heeded the voice of Jonathan, and Saul swore, "*As* the LORD lives, he shall not be killed." Then Jonathan called David, and Jonathan told him all these things. So Jonathan brought David to Saul, and he was in his presence as in times past (verses 3-7).

I have seen torn relationships in a church, and I realize that if we were the good friends we claim to be, when we see our friends separated from another, we would intercede. It is possible to put our arms around two friends and, in doing so, bring them together.

3. It Always Faces Trouble

Friendship always faces trouble, and always stands in the place of one who is hurting. Consider what happened when Jonathan's friendship with David was tested:

> So Jonathan answered Saul, "David earnestly asked *permission* of me *to go* to Bethlehem. And he said, 'Please let me go, for our family has a sacrifice in the city, and my brother has commanded me *to be there.* And now, if I have found favor in your eyes, please let me get away and see my brothers.' Therefore he has not come to the king's table." Then Saul's anger was aroused against Jonathan, and he said to him, "You son of a perverse, rebellious *woman*! Do I not know that you have chosen the son of Jesse to your own shame and to the shame of your mother's nakedness? For as long as the son of Jesse lives on the earth, you shall not be established, nor your kingdom. Now, therefore, send and bring him to me, for he shall surely die." And Jonathan answered Saul his father, and said to him, "Why should he be killed? What has he done?" Then Saul cast a spear at him to kill him, by which Jonathan knew that it was determined by his father to kill David. So Jonathan arose from the table in fierce anger, and ate no food the second day of the month, for he was grieved for David, because his father had treated him shamefully (1 Samuel 20:28-34).

What a great example Jonathan sets for us! David knew his relationship with Jonathan was secure because Jonathan was willing to stand up to his own father on his behalf.

Christ's Committed Friendship With Us

It makes me feel good to think about having a friend like that. I have two men who are my best and closest friends, men to whom I could tell anything that is in my heart. But I also have a friend to whom I can unburden my soul at any time, day or night, who understands me better than I understand myself; when I pour out my heart to Him, He is always there for me. That friend is the Lord Jesus Christ. He is my most important friend, and I'm not sure anyone can really dispel the loneliness without knowing Him.

He Selected Us

When I read about the friendship of David and Jonathan, I think of the relationship I have with the Lord. Jesus selected me; He chose me to be His own. I wasn't looking for Him. In fact, I was running away from Him. But He chose me to be His own child, and now I belong to Him.

He Sacrificed for Us

As Jonathan sacrificed for David, so Jesus sacrificed for me. He came down out of the throne room of glory, turning His back on the riches of His kingdom in order to save me. He took off the royal robes that were His by right and clothed me with His own royal robes, making me part of the family of God. He eventually gave His own life in order that I might go free. Jesus loved me with a sacrificial love. He paid the greatest price ever.

His Steadfast Friendship With His Father

Jonathan was able to maintain his relationship with his father, and Jesus was able to maintain His relationship with the Heavenly Father, facing the fact that His Father would one day turn His back upon Him. In order for Jesus to be my friend, He had to identify with me and on the cross bear my sin. He was willing to be forsaken by His Father in order that He might reach down and accept me as His friend. He reached up with one hand and took hold of a holy God and then reached down with the other and took hold of sinful man. In dying on the cross, He brought the two together. Jesus Christ is the embodiment of steadfast love.

He Gives Security

There are three ways Christ provides security:

1. He Warns of Judgment

As Jonathan brought security to David, so Jesus brings security to me.

2. He Intercedes in Trouble

He warns me of judgment and intercedes for me in times of trouble.

3. He Takes My Punishment

I am absolutely secure for eternity because of Jesus Christ. He is truly my committed friend.

1. Who is your closest friend? Or do you have multiple committed friends?

   a. What brought you together?

   b. What common traits do you possess? How do they draw you closer to each other?

   c. What differences do you possess? How do you make sure your differences are not bigger than your love and respect for each other?

   d. If you only have one committed friend, how does that friendship differ from the other friends you have?

e. How long have you known your closest friend? What trials and tests has your relationship endured? Was it ultimately strengthened? Why or why not?

2. In this lesson, you learned not only about committed friends but also about the characteristics that exist in a relationship with such a person. Does your most committed friendship possess some of these traits?

   a. If you have chosen one special person in your life to be your committed friend, how can the two of you gain the traits discussed in this lesson?

   b. In what ways is your friendship already selective, sacrificial, steadfast, and secure?

   c. What areas can use a bit more dedication this week?

3. A committed friend in your life can minister to you in many ways, but even that friendship is meant to serve as a reminder that Jesus Christ is an even closer friend.

   a. What are three things you're appreciative of in your relationship with Jesus?

   b. What does your relationship with Jesus teach you about being selective in your friendships with other people?

   c. How does your relationship with Jesus challenge you to love more deeply and to be more committed to others?

4. In your opinion, what makes a great friend? How do you measure up to those statistics?

1. What were we taught about friendship when we were children?

   a. What friends stuck with us as we grew up?

   b. What are the characteristics of those friendships?

2. Who served as examples of a committed friendship when finding friends was a cause of confusion for us?

3. In Scripture, we're given Jesus' wisdom about friendship when He tells the disciples that love means to "lay down one's life for his friends" (John 15:13).

   a. Why was Jesus an authority on this type of love?

4. In this lesson, we learned about the sacrificial love of our Savior —He was our rejected Lord.

   a. What was Jesus trying to communicate to us in His willingness to make the ultimate sacrifice at the cross?

5. For many people, a spouse is the only committed friend they want or have. How can we make sure our marriages are truly committed friendships?

   a. How can we be the selective, sacrificial, steadfast, and secure partner our spouse needs?

6. The human cure for loneliness can be as close as a text message or phone call away when you have a committed friend. How have our friendships served as a relief from loneliness?

a. Have we gained stronger friendships from times of loneliness? How?

b. If we haven't had a significant season of loneliness ourselves, how have we been an encouragement to our friends?

7. If we feel alone, how can we ask God to bring a committed friend into our lives?

a. What should we do to build a stronger connection to other people in our times of loneliness?

DID YOU KNOW?

In John 15:13, Jesus said, "Greater love has no one than this, than to lay down one's life for his friends." Jesus showed the greatest love of all in dying for us, His friends, on the cross.

GOD'S HEAVENLY CURE FOR LONELINESS

Psalm 142

In this lesson we'll sum up what we've learned and offer a cure for the lonely Christian.

OUTLINE

During one particularly trying time, David was lonely and discouraged. He was abandoned by friends, King Saul was after him, and he worried for his very life. In the midst of the trial, David poured out his heart to God. The words he wrote reveal a way out of our loneliness.

I. **David Describes His Problem of Loneliness**
   A. He Is Disoriented
   B. He Is Deserted
   C. He Is Depressed
   D. He Is Defeated

II. **David Defines the Solution to Loneliness**
   A. He Verbalized the Problem
   B. He Visualized the Problem
   C. He Recognized the Problem
   D. He Realized His Provision
   E. He Summarized His Victory

Not long ago I read an article by a man leaving the ministry. He complained that as his church had grown, the demands on his time had become incredible. His children grew up without really knowing him, and he felt alone and isolated in his role as counselor. Eventually his spiritual life began to dry up. Though on the outside everything looked great, on the inside he felt like he was a failure. After eighteen years, he decided to quit his pastorate, unsure if he had what it takes to be a leader. I find that a sad story, though not too uncommon. The words are not too different from those found in Psalm 142, where the author cries out in loneliness for help from God. That psalm offers a wonderful presentation of the cycle of discouragement through which every person travels at some time in life.

There are marginal notes at the top of this psalm which tell us it was written by David when he was in a cave. That helps us understand what was going on in the author's life when he put the words to paper. As you look back in history, you discover that there are two special cave stories in the life of David. In 1 Samuel 24, David was in hiding from King Saul in the cave of Engedi. During his search for David, King Saul went into that very cave to relieve himself, and David secretly cut off a part of Saul's garment. He later waved it at the king, as a way of showing that he could have killed Saul, had he chosen to do so. Instead, David had allowed the king to live. The grace of David's actions shamed Saul into taking his soldiers and going home.

The other time David was in a cave—the experience which caused him to write Psalm 142—is described in 1 Samuel 22. David is again running from King Saul, who is jealous and trying to kill his arch rival. After chasing him all over the countryside, we find these words:

> David therefore departed from there and escaped to the cave of Adullam. So when his brothers and all his father's house heard *it*, they went down there to him. And everyone *who was* in distress, everyone who was in debt, and everyone *who was* discontented gathered to him. So he became captain over them. And there were about four hundred men with him (1 Samuel 22:1–2).

A distressed David, surrounded by the debtors and discontented of Israel, found himself hiding in the cave of Adullam. In the midst of his anger and fear, David wrote these words:

I cry out to the LORD with my voice; with my voice to the LORD I make my supplication. I pour out my complaint before Him; I declare before Him my trouble. When my spirit was overwhelmed within me, then You knew my path. In the way in which I walk they have secretly set a snare for me. Look on *my* right hand and see, for *there is* no one who acknowledges me; refuge has failed me; no one cares for my soul. I cried out to You, O LORD: I said, "You *are* my refuge, my portion in the land of the living. Attend to my cry, for I am brought very low; deliver me from my persecutors, for they are stronger than I. Bring my soul out of prison, that I may praise Your name; the righteous shall surround me, for You shall deal bountifully with me" (Psalm 142).

DAVID DESCRIBES HIS PROBLEM OF LONELINESS

It might seem strange that David would speak of loneliness when he is surrounded by 400 people, but consider the sort of people around him. They weren't folks he could confide in. They weren't any comfort to him. And they weren't soldiers, to protect him in his refuge. So when David sat down to write, he described how he felt at the time; it gives us a window not only into the man but into the emotions of all lonely people. I've read dozens of books on loneliness, and nothing comes close to capturing the beauty of language and the emotional overtones of David's descriptions. Reflect for a few moments on what David was feeling.

He Is Disoriented

"My spirit was overwhelmed," David says. The words literally mean,"my spirit was muffled." It is as though a fierce flood of emotions has rushed down upon him. His trouble and gloom have smothered him, and he is simply trying to reach out and express himself. At this point, David has lost his way. He is totally disoriented, and doesn't know which way to turn. Loneliness can make us confused.

He Is Deserted

David says in verse 4 that there is no one beside him. Even though there were 400 other people, he didn't feel there was anyone close to him. He felt abandoned, rejected, and isolated. Pursued by a jealous king, left alone by his friends, and having to hide in a cave caused David to feel completely alone. Many lonely people share that feeling of desertion.

He Is Depressed

The result of those feelings can be found in verse 6: "I am brought very low." The words literally mean that David was going into a valley. It was an emotional low point for him, the low ebb of his life. All his joy is gone, his hope evaporated. He could think of nothing positive to say about his future. David was at the very bottom, depressed about his circumstance and his life. That is the very picture of many people's lives. They feel alone, they don't know what to do, and the result is they suffer deep depression.

He Is Defeated

It is one thing to be depressed and to have hope for things getting better someday, but it is another to look forward and believe that things will never change. That's how David was feeling—totally defeated by his circumstances. He sees that all of those around him are stronger than he is, and he realizes that he does not have the strength in his band of followers to fight the powers arrayed against them. It's as though David feels the walls closing in around him, and there is no way of escape. Doom is just around the corner. That feeling of defeat is common when we're feeling lonely. Sometimes feelings of defeat even occur in the lives of those in leadership, as their servanthood or position isolates them from other people. Older people often feel this way as they realize there is no way to defeat the process of aging, or as they face sickness that so often accompanies age. Those who have been hurt can also feel defeated. The breakup of a marriage or relationship, having to move to a new city, or being separated from the ones we love can simply cause us to feel defeated. There is a sadness, a loneliness, that steals over us and saps our strength. That's exactly how David felt as he hid in his cave, pondering his situation.

DAVID DEFINES THE SOLUTION TO LONELINESS

But there is good news in all this: David doesn't simply describe his feelings, he also offers a clue as to how we can deal with those feelings. Psalm 142 offers a formula for dealing with loneliness—God's heavenly cure. If we will look closely, we can find the solution for dealing with loneliness.

He Verbalized the Problem

The first thing to notice is that David talked about how he felt. He verbalized his feelings. Note how carefully the Scripture records that David cried out to the Lord with his voice, poured out his complaint, and described his trouble to God. He didn't let it build up inside him, but over and over he expressed his feelings to the Lord. The words, "I cried out to God" may sound trite in a psalm, but they are the first step to healing a lonely heart. We must be able to go honestly before God and say, "Lord, these are the feelings within me. I'm opening up my heart to You because I want You to know how I feel." Too often our prayers are benign. We come to God with pious platitudes, doing all of our praying on the surface while deep down we are hurting desperately. Somehow we neglect to tell the best friend we have in the world, the One who created and redeemed us, about the cry of our heart. One of the things that David teaches me is that it is all right to tell God how I feel. That's the start of healing.

Talking with a friend is often therapeutic. There is a little book by Joseph Bayly entitled *The Psalms of My Life* which tells of a man spending time in a motel away from his family. He prays, telling the Lord of his sorrow at being alone, and admitting that he doesn't feel very spiritual about being lonely. And you know, God isn't surprised at that sort of honesty. Our Heavenly Father already knows how we feel. The Holy Spirit is a friend, caring enough about us that He is willing to cry out in anguish at the loneliness of our soul. When we verbalize our feelings to God, we are simply getting them out in the open where God can meet our need and help us deal with them.

I remember the first time I had the courage to audibly tell the Lord, "I don't really feel like talking to You today. I want to feel that way, but I don't." And I found that God could meet me where I was, and help me to change. But if I denied how I was feeling, I was lying to the Lord, and He couldn't help me. Verbalizing our feelings to Him is the first step in defeating loneliness.

He Visualized the Problem

David notes that he let his prayer "be set free . . . as incense." The King James Version translates that as "pour[ing] out my complaint before Him." In other words, David didn't just describe how he felt, but painted God a picture. He made clear where he was, talking about the discontented and debtors in his midst, and laying out the whole sordid mess for the Lord. "Take a look at this," David says to God. "This is what my life is like."

I know how David feels. You should see some of the pictures I've painted for God. That's not because it is good for God, but because it is good for me. It is a good thing to visualize your problems, for it helps you keep them in perspective. For example, do you remember when Israel sent twelve spies into Kadesh Barnea? They went over to look at the Promised Land; when they came back, the two groups painted two different pictures. The majority of those reporting spoke of giants in the land, and claimed that the people would be "like grasshoppers" before them. The picture they painted was one of big trouble. But Joshua and Caleb also reported, painting a picture of a land "flowing with milk and honey." They didn't forget the giants, but they didn't paint themselves as grasshoppers, either. They made sure to make God part of the picture.

I've often seen lonely people paint their problems as bigger than God, but God is greater than any circumstance we face. So when you are feeling lonely, verbalize how you feel, and visualize your circumstances to the Lord. Allow Him to keep your situation in perspective.

He Recognized the Problem

David recognized that God already knew about his troubles. "When my spirit was overwhelmed within me, then You knew my path" (verse 3). We don't so much inform God as let Him know that we recognize our own struggles. We don't have to come before God tentatively, as though we aren't sure if we should tell Him or not—He already knows. It isn't hard to tell someone hard news if they already know about it, and the Bible tells us over and over again that God knows all about us. When we come to visualize and verbalize our problem of loneliness before Him, we need to recognize that He already knows and understands. What a comfort to know that we don't surprise the Lord, and what a comfort it instills in us when we pray!

He Realized His Provision

Once we recognize that God already knows everything about us, we must realize what we have in Him. Our God is bigger than our circumstances, stronger than our problems, our refuge in a storm. David realized that God is greater than his immediate concerns.

When Daniel's three friends were thrown into the fiery furnace, everyone looked into the flames and saw someone with them. God would not allow His children to go through something like that alone. He will never leave us or forsake us. Isaiah the prophet puts it this way:

But now, thus says the LORD, who created you, O Jacob,
and He who formed you, O Israel: "Fear not, for I have
redeemed you; I have called *you* by your name; you *are*
Mine. When you pass through the waters, I *will be* with
you; and through the rivers, they shall not overflow you.
When you walk through the fire, you shall not be burned,
nor shall the flame scorch you. For I *am* the LORD your God,
the Holy One of Israel, your Savior" (Isaiah 43:1–3).

I particularly like the fact that God will go "through" those
experiences with us—in other words, they will have an end. We
will get to the other side. Our troubles won't last forever. The God
who is our refuge and our portion has promised to get us on the
other side of the lonely, difficult experience. That's what David
realized. We have the Almighty God of the universe on our side.

He Summarized His Victory

At the end of Psalm 142, David summarized his victory. "Bring
my soul out of prison," he writes, "that I may praise Your name."
David prayed for an end, knowing that his God was greater than his
circumstances. "The righteous shall surround me, for You shall deal
bountifully with me." From crying in anguish, David moved to a
confidence in God's ability to make things right. He knew one day
God would encourage him with faithful and supportive friends, and
that the Lord would bless him.

Many Christians try to get to verse 7 without walking through all
the prior verses. We try to make ourselves strong and stand tall and,
instead of honestly dealing with the issues, we pretend that everything
is all right. Don't get me wrong; I don't think we need to remain in
verses 1–3. But at the same time, we have to understand that it takes
a while to get through our situations. In an immediate world, we
need to allow God to slowly use time to heal us. It's not wrong to be
in difficult straits. We all go through them. But we need to be willing
to swallow our pride and approach the Lord for His help.

If you are lonely, remember that David was there before you.
God gave us his story so that we would know what to do and how
to respond to achieve victory over loneliness. We can let go of all
that is burdening us and allow God to help us struggle through
the problem.

1. David went through a constant cycle of healing. What can his story teach you about the steps you need to take with God in order to heal?

    a. Confessing and confiding were big parts of David's healing. Why are they important steps toward healing?

    b. Is it possible to heal without pouring your heart out to God in prayer? Why or why not?

    c. What can God teach you when you confide your deepest and truest feelings to Him?

    d. What is there to gain from being honest with God?

2. What is causing your loneliness right now?

    a. Is it more important for you to understand why you are lonely, or to use this time to draw near to Christ? Why?

    b. What can you do in your season of loneliness that would bring healing, even if this healing doesn't cure your pain?

3. What does healing look like for you in your situation?

    a. Has your loneliness pulled you away from God or has your relationship with Him been strengthened?

    b. What comfort do you find in knowing that God already knows what you need?

c. What do you think God desires for you in this season?

4. How has God met you in this season?

    a. Is it easier now to be honest with God about the matters of your heart? Why or why not?

    b. What have you gained in your relationship with Him that you didn't previously have?

5. How does the heavenly cure for loneliness differ from the human cure for loneliness?

    a. Are they similar or vastly different? Why or why not?

1. The last two lessons taught us about two cures for loneliness: one where we can rely on others in friendship, and the other where we can fully rely on God because He knows what we need.

    a. Does one cure make the loneliness more bearable than the other? Or are they equal? Why?

    b. How has God used both cures in our seasons of loneliness?

    c. What has each cure taught us about God's heart and love for us?

2. Sometimes it can be difficult for us to open our hearts to the Lord, even though He already has an intimate knowledge of what we are feeling. We should remember that He desires for us to talk to Him.

a. What should be our expectation when approaching Him?

b. Should we only pour out our hearts so we can get something from Him? Or should our goal be to draw closer to Him and seek His comfort? Why?

c. Why does God desire our honesty when we are suffering?

3. Looking back on your lonely seasons, what has God revealed about yourself? List three things God taught you in the context of your relationship with Him and your relationships with others:

a.

b.

c.

4. What has God revealed about Himself in this season of loneliness?

    a. What can you confidently say about God's attributes which have been shown to you (His love, mercy, kindness, gentleness, etc.) during this season?

    b. How can you use this confidence to not doubt God when life gets difficult and lonely?

5. How can we utilize what we have learned from our seasons of loneliness to ultimately draw people closer to the God of all comfort?

DID YOU KNOW?

What we call the book of Psalms is actually five books of hymns and poems, originally written in Hebrew. If you'll look at the margin notes in your Bible, you'll see that it divides the book into five parts before Psalms 1, 42, 73, 90, and 107.

Overcoming Loneliness

Loneliness may well be the prevailing disease of our time. No one, married or single, religious or non-religious, young or old, is exempt from the pain. Though we are all susceptible to loneliness at some point in our lives, we can overcome it and fill that aching void. In *Overcoming Loneliness*, Dr. Jeremiah points out several positive methods for healing this disease of the soul. This is the perfect resource not only to encourage you but to help you know how to help others overcome the bondage of loneliness.

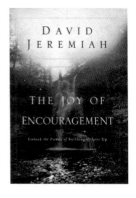

The Joy of Encouragement
Unlock the Power of Building Others Up

Dr. Jeremiah examines the heart of self-giving, genuine love—and suggests helpful ways to learn to express the kind of encouragement that heals, unites, and renews people's zest for life. Scriptural and uplifting, *The Joy of Encouragement* has the potential to radically reshape the world and to equip people as ambassadors of the God of love.

Courage to Conquer

How did the Bible's greatest heroes confront life's challenges and conquer with courage? In *Courage to Conquer*, Dr. Jeremiah introduces you to these heroes and shares the source of their strength. When you discover the Source of their strength and make Him the strength of your life, you too can face life with the courage to conquer.

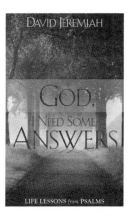

God, I Need Some Answers
Life Lessons from Psalms

Some questions seem to plague us. But there is hope. God has revealed Himself in His Word through stories and poetry about real people in real situations. God is not afraid of our questions or our doubts; in fact, He longs to answer them. Dr. Jeremiah's selection of several Psalms guides our discovery of the answers to ten tough questions Christians ask.

Each of these resources was created from a teaching series by Dr. David Jeremiah. Contact Turning Point for more information about correlating materials.

For pricing information and ordering, contact us at

with Dr. David Jeremiah

P.O. Box 3838
San Diego, CA 92163
(800) 947-1993
www.DavidJeremiah.org

STAY CONNECTED
to Dr. David Jeremiah

Take advantage of two great ways to let Dr. David Jeremiah give you spiritual direction every day!

Turning Points Magazine and Devotional

Receive Dr. David Jeremiah's magazine, *Turning Points*, each month:

- Thematic study focus
- 48 pages of life-changing reading
- Relevant articles
- Special features
- Daily devotional readings
- Bible study resource offers
- Live event schedule
- Radio & television information

Request *Turning Points* magazine today!

(800) 947-1993
www.DavidJeremiah.org/Magazine

Daily Turning Point E-Devotional

Start your day off right! Find words of inspiration and spiritual motivation waiting for you on your computer every morning! Receive a daily e-devotion communication from David Jeremiah that will strengthen your walk with God and encourage you to live the authentic Christian life.

Request your free e-devotional today!

(800) 947-1993
www.DavidJeremiah.org/Devo